Praise ... Mindfulness fo

'Mind. ... lusive ... The 'I'm too busy' thoughts snow up and get in the way. The trick is to bring brief respites of mindfulness into a multitude of simple tasks we do each day. In this second edition of their wonderful book the authors have added, updated and upgraded ideas for bringing the power of mindfulness into our busy worlds. Get it and reap the benefits of simple mindfulness.'

Kevin Polk, PhD, Psychologist and ProSocial Matrix Trainer

'The great thing is, we can all be a lot more mindful, even if we're way too busy to meditate. This little gem of a book gives you a wealth of simple strategies to easily bring mindfulness into everyday life, thereby making it a lot more satisfying and lot less stressful.'

Russ Harris, author, *The Happiness Trap*

'Mindfulness has probably become more popular in concept than in practice these days. So many of us could benefit from training our attention and our self-compassion, if we could just find practical ways to integrate mindfulness into our daily lives and busy schedules. These authors provide the practical tools that you need to actually put mindfulness into practice, and to benefit from transforming your mind, without having to pack up to live in the mountains. This book is fun, usable, and helpful.'

Dennis Tirch, author, *The Compassionate Mind Guide to Overcoming Anxiety*

'Accessible, actionable, insightful and user-friendly. This book will help even the busiest of people find more contentment, joy, calm and connection especially on the busiest of days.'

Aisling Leonard-Curtin, Chartered Psychologist; Co-director, ACT Now Purposeful Living; author, *The Power of Small*

'Fun, engaging and practical – this book is elegantly written by experts to help you learn the skills of mindfulness – and to apply them to this busy, stressful, modern world we live in.'

Joe Oliver, Director of Contextual Consulting; co-author, *ACTivate Your Life*

'Read, practise and feel the rewards – this accessible book has the power to change your life.'

Mary Welford, author, *Compassionate Mind Approach to Building Self-Confidence* and *Compassion Focused Therapy for Dummies*

'A lot of people would like to learn to live more mindfully, but feel they simply don't have the time. The second edition of *Mindfulness for Busy People* shows us how to bring the benefits of mindfulness into the busiest of lives.'

Russell Kolts, PhD, Professor of Psychology, Eastern Washington University; co-author, *Living with an Open Heart: How to Cultivate Compassion in Everyday Life*

'One go-to question in mindfulness is: What did you notice? Going through this wonderful book, I noticed how simple and concrete it made the practice of mindfulness. I noticed thoughts about wishing I had come across this book when I first encountered mindfulness some 18 years ago. Then, I noticed warm feelings toward the compassionate humanity of Mike Sinclair, Josie Seydel and Emily Shaw that shines through each page. The next thing I noticed was loving how this new edition delves on self-compassion and offers more on how mindfulness can help us identify, choose and embody our deepest life values. Finally, I noticed the judgment that this book isn't just for busy people, but for anyone interested in living more effectively and learning how to befriend the whole of their experience.'

Benjamin Schoendorff, co-author, *The Science of Compassion and The Essential Guide to the ACT Matrix.*

'Having read this new edition, I doubt I will ever again notice my mind telling me "I'd better watch the time" without recalling the "watch your watch" meditation – just one of a plethora of mini life practice suggestions in this accessible self-helper that contribute to busting through the self-inflicted aspect of the trance of "too busy"ness.'

Marin Wilks, Chartered Psychologist, mindfulness teacher, peer-reviewed ACT Trainer

'This book is an incredibly practical guide to reducing stress and boosting your effectiveness through mindfulness.'

Rob Yeung, Chartered Psychologist; author, *Confidence 2.0: The New Science of Self-Confidence*

Praise for the first edition

'A highly practical and engaging book. Recommended reading for just about everybody and anybody.'

Russ Harris, author, *The Happiness Trap*

'An operating manual for the most important but least understood area of our lives – the mind and how we think. Good for thinking about business, great for thinking about life and living it.'

Paul Ward, investment banker and CEO

'An engaging and amusing read that covers a highly important topic: Awareness and Acceptance as core tenets of mental health. The exercises are easily identifiable, humorous and relevant.'

Peter Lawrence, Financial Analyst

'Mindfulness offers a practical and simple approach to becoming more confident and effective in today's busy workplace.'

Stephney Dallmann, Director, Professional Services Firm

'As a CEO, I often turn to the mindfulness techniques as outlined in this book to create the psychological "still space" I need for considered analysis and calm reflection on business issues. The techniques allow timely, confident decision making to flow naturally out of even the most complex and fast moving situations.'

Raza Khan, CEO, Buckinghamshire Learning Trust

Mindfulness for Busy People

 Pearson

Harlow, England • London • New York • Boston • San Francisco • Toronto • Sydney • Dubai • Singapore • Hong Kong
Tokyo • Seoul • Taipei • New Delhi • Cape Town • São Paulo • Mexico City • Madrid • Amsterdam • Munich • Paris • Milan

Pearson

At Pearson, we have a simple mission: to help people
make more of their lives through learning.

We combine innovative learning technology with trusted
content and educational expertise to provide engaging
and effective learning experiences that serve people
wherever and whenever they are learning.

From classroom to boardroom, our curriculum materials, digital
learning tools and testing programmes help to educate millions
of people worldwide – more than any other private enterprise.

Every day our work helps learning flourish, and
wherever learning flourishes, so do people.

To learn more, please visit us at **www.pearson.com/uk**

MICHAEL SINCLAIR, JOSIE SEYDEL
AND EMILY SHAW

Mindfulness for Busy People

Turning from frantic and frazzled
into calm and composed

SECOND EDITION

Harlow, England • London • New York • Boston • San Francisco • Toronto • Sydney • Dubai • Singapore • Hong Kong
Tokyo • Seoul • Taipei • New Delhi • Cape Town • São Paulo • Mexico City • Madrid • Amsterdam • Munich • Paris • Milan

PEARSON EDUCATION LIMITED
KAO Two
KAO Park
Harlow
CM17 9NA
United Kingdom
Tel: +44 (0)1279 623623
Web: www.pearson.com/uk

First published 2013 (print and electronic)
Second edition published 2018 (print and electronic)

ISBN: 978-1-292-18640-5 (print)
          978-1-292-18691-7 (PDF)
          978-1-292-18692-4 (ePub)

British Library Cataloguing-in-Publication Data
A catalogue record for the print edition is available from the British Library

Library of Congress Cataloging-in-Publication Data
A catalog record for the print edition is available from the Library of Congress

10 9 8 7 6 5 4 3 2 1
22 21 20 19 18

Cartoons by Stu McLellan
Cover design by Two Associates
Print edition typeset in 10/12pt ITC Giovanni Std by SPi Global
Print edition printed and bound in Great Britain by Ashford Colour Press Ltd.

NOTE THAT ANY PAGE CROSS REFERENCES REFER TO THE PRINT EDITION

Contents

About the authors

Michael Sinclair is a consultant counselling psychologist, an associate fellow of the British Psychological Society and the clinical director of City Psychology Group in London. His clinical work is influenced by Contextual Behavioural Science and he has expertise in delivering a range of mindfulness-based interventions. He is an experienced practitioner of Acceptance and Commitment Therapy (ACT) and has taught mindfulness to hundreds of people over many years. He has been dedicated to his own mindfulness practice for over 12 years. Michael continues to provide the highest quality psychological therapy and coaching to individuals of all ages, couples and families.

He is the consultant to a number of corporate occupational health departments in the City of London, assisting with employees' stress management and well-being. He delivers mindfulness-based workshops to corporate executives, as well as larger public audiences, and is actively involved in teaching mindfulness to practising psychologists and other health professionals. He is the author of a range of self-help books.

Michael has been inspired by the many people he has met through his work as a practitioner psychologist over the past 17 years. He has worked with children, those suffering with life-threatening medical diagnoses and illnesses (and their loved ones), celebrities and senior business leaders. He has become fascinated by the shared experience and common universal themes and psychological processes met in each of us and the human resilience to survive in the face of extreme adversity. He is privileged to have been able help hundreds of people to discover and tap into this resilience, sense of shared humanity and wisdom, to cultivate these incredible qualities and to find a genuine sense of well-being. He hopes that this book will go some way in doing the same for you.

Josie Seydel was first taught to meditate at the age of ten and remembers sitting in the car with her family silently reciting mantras. Given this experience, it is not surprising that she chose to become a psychologist and continue to work on understanding what the heck that was all about. At the age of 18, Josie learned mindfulness meditation, hung out with hippies, travelled about and discovered that to find herself (wherever she was) she needed only to breathe.

She became a chartered counselling psychologist in 2003 and is now also an associate fellow of the British Psychological Society. She has worked in several different and diverse settings during her career, including: specialist eating disorders services, refugee and asylum seeker services, domestic violence services, women's prisons, adolescent in-patient services and primary schools. Everywhere she has gone she has found real human beings, from the highest corporate lawyers to the most dejected and shunned murderers, all also able to breathe and find themselves (with a little help) and to see that we are not so very different after all.

She currently works as a clinical associate with City Psychology Group, in the City of London, providing mindfulness-based psychological therapy to people of all ages as well as pioneering mindfulness workshops to large public audiences. Josie is also the mother of two young children and so understands stress quite well. Through her compassionate and committed professional and personal dedication to practice she continues to marvel that mindfulness truly allows the heart to find ease. May you find this, too.

Emily Shaw is a chartered clinical psychologist, working as a clinical executive at City Psychology Group and also works in the NHS with people who experience complex mental health difficulties. When Emily first heard about mindfulness, many years ago, she was sceptical of how something so simple could be so beneficial to so many. She then met a number of people she admired who convinced her to give it a go. Being a very busy person herself, she found brief practices were a good place to start and now a day does not pass without many mindful moments, helping her to feel a greater sense of ease.

She is committed to a lifelong journey of mindfulness practice and is passionate about sharing her wisdom with the people she works with. She hopes this book inspires you to practise in a way that works for you, so that you may find kindness for yourself and all other beings.

Acknowledgements

We are deeply grateful to the many mindfulness based researchers and therapists who we have had the honour to work with and learn from over the years; your wisdom and passion inspire us. Thank you to all of our clients, who have taught us the most; without you this book would not have been possible. Finally, with heartfelt gratitude to all our loved ones for their unwavering support and love. May you all find joy, peace and ease in your life.

We and the publisher would like to thank Stu McLellan for his wonderful illustrations (www.stumclellan.co.uk).

Introduction

What we will cover in this book and how to use it

In this book, we are keen to:

▶ show you how mindfulness can dramatically improve your busy life.

▶ teach you some ways to practise mindfulness that are especially easy to fit into your busy life, without *changing anything* in your life.

▶ illustrate to you just how accessible mindfulness is to you, and how opportunities to practise it are abundant and infinite, despite how busy you are.

▶ show you how being mindfully compassionate towards yourself can help you to handle your busy life with greater ease and effectiveness.

▶ show you how to cultivate less stress and more well-being and efficiency in any given moment of your busy life.

▶ help you get in touch with what matters most to you and to build more of the life that you want for yourself.

We have designed this book as a guide to practising mindfulness on-the-go. We will help you to learn how to better manage your busyness, creating space when it feels like you are suffocating under the never-ending jobs you have to do. It is easy to think of mindfulness as yet another futile time-consumer, but you will soon see how it is really an effective time-saver. In fact, our own experience, and a growing body of research, tells us that the busier we are the more we may need and benefit from mindfulness.

Whether you choose to spend more or less time on your mindfulness practice is absolutely fine, as evidence shows that even practising just a few minutes a day can have a positive impact – although the more mindfulness practice you do, the more you notice the benefits.

The book is divided into five parts, which we believe will provide you with a good starting point for your onward journey of mindfulness practice. However, if you are already familiar with mindfulness, we hope that this book will inspire you to try new ways of practising and keep your practice going. Feel free to pause between each part for as long as you need, to give yourself time to practise as much as you like. If you prefer to read straight through the book, then go ahead. You can always revisit parts and any of the practices again.

This book is full of practical mindfulness practices, designed to fit into your busy life. For quick reference and easy accessibility, you will find them dotted throughout the book, under the following headings:

▶ **I haven't got time for this!** These exercises are designed for you to practise throughout your busy day. They are focused on everyday activities that, likely, you will be doing anyway and can, therefore, be incorporated as you go about your busyness.

▶ **Mindfulness right now!** These exercises are for when you can spare a few moments as you are reading the book and are designed to help you reflect on the principles that we are keen to share with you.

Salient learning points are summarised at the end of each chapter, under the heading **Mindfulness top tips to-go.**

Finally, to support your mindfulness practice, at the end of each part, we have suggested various practices that you can try out and reflect on that have been covered in the book. There is no right or wrong way to practise and we would not expect everyone to do all the suggested practices in one go, so we recommend that you pick whatever feels manageable for you. Take mindfulness at your own pace, allowing it to become a natural part of your life – there is no rush! Incorporating mindfulness in a way that suits you personally will mean that it will become a normal part of your everyday experience.

Audio recordings are also included, which will assist you as a guide through certain practices (should you want to use them), and they are indicated by this symbol:

You can download the audio guides for free from:
www.pearson-books.com/mindfulness

Why is this book full of practical exercises you may ask? Well, we can tell you all about mindfulness and you can appreciate, understand and grasp it – but, unless you practise, it will not make the slightest difference to your life! Rather than only taking our word on this, here is what the late Steve Jobs had to say on the subject:

> 'If you just sit and observe, you will see how restless your mind is,' Jobs told his biographer, Walter Isaacson. 'If you try to calm it, it only makes it worse, but over time it does calm, and when it does, there's room to hear more subtle things – that's when your intuition starts to blossom and you start to see things more clearly and be in the present more. Your mind just slows down, and you see a tremendous expanse in the moment. You see so much more than you could see before. *It's a discipline; you have to practise it.'*

The late Steve Jobs – former co-founder, chairman and CEO of Apple Inc.

The benefits of mindfulness

You may have picked this book up because you are interested to learn more about mindfulness generally, what it can do for you and maybe how you could incorporate it into your busy life. Or you may simply be just so crazy busy right now and at your absolute wits' end that you are willing to give anything a try (mindfulness or whatever it may take!) to find some relief and peace and quiet from your frantic existence. Either way, you have come to the right place – this book is for you.

As busy people ourselves, we are all too familiar with what it is like to be rushed off your feet, scrambling around, constantly on the go, never feeling like everything is done, that there is never enough time in the day, feeling tired, exhausted, stressed out and fed up most of the time. We also understand how frustrating it is to be told just to think positively, just to take some time simply to switch off and relax, to delegate more to others and to get better at prioritising our daily tasks and improve our time management skills.

Well, if, like us, you have tried all this, then you have probably also found that it just does not work and it is just not that simple. Thankfully, we have discovered something that is always there to help us manage our hectic lives, something that really does work, and that is something called mindfulness.

As practising psychologists in the City of London, we provide mindfulness-based therapy and coaching sessions and also run mindfulness, stress management, resilience and well-being workshops for very busy people just like you (and us), and we are keen to share some of the techniques and expert guidance that we use in our work with our clients and in our own personal lives every day; techniques that really do work to help you be more in control of your busy day. If you then choose to practise mindfulness regularly, then let us warn you – it *will* change your life (in a good way).

Specifically, by practising mindfulness regularly you can expect to:

▶ improve your motivation and energy levels.

▶ be more focused and therefore more productive and effective.

▶ boost your immune system and improve your general health

▶ decrease your stress and chances of other mental health problems.

▶ enhance your communication skills and enjoy more fulfilling relationships.

▶ respond to your own and the emotions of others with greater understanding and kindness.

▶ create a more enjoyable, meaningful and fulfilling life.

We are not here to sell you false promises; all these benefits are yours for the taking. You will, however, need to practise mindfulness to notice them happening for you – and we are going to show you just how to do this throughout this book, without necessarily needing to find any extra time in your busy day.

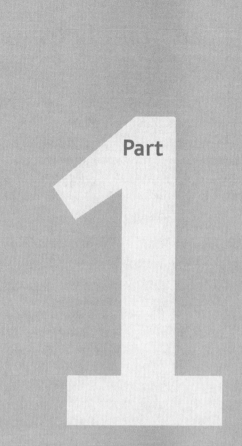

Part

1

Mindfulness and me

In the first part of the book we are keen to:

▶ Introduce you to mindfulness, its origins and uses.

▶ Explain what mindfulness is and isn't all about.

▶ Help you understand why and how mindfulness can be relevant and helpful in these stressful and busy, modern times.

▶ Show you how you don't need to change what you do in your life to practise or benefit from mindfulness.

▶ Show you how to start practising mindfulness.

How can mindfulness change your life?

Mindfulness has been introduced to the Western world over the past several decades in medical, health, educational, family and business settings. Mindfulness has caught on a storm and is rapidly gathering a great deal of evidence-based support and media attention. This is partly because it is so accessible and simple to learn; it is not a technique restricted by culture, religion, gender, age, educational level, physical or mental health or disability (beyond the most extreme) or wealth. Also it actually works!

Evidence for the benefits and value of mindfulness in the Western world is not actually as new as it might at first seem under the recent boom in popularity. For example, Jon Kabat-Zinn, who has written many books (see the section Recommended reading), began his research with some fabulous work using mindfulness as part of a stress-reduction programme in Massachusetts. This programme began in the late 1970s to help lots of people manage their stress, anxiety, pain and illness. He wrote:

> Most people come to the clinic because they want to relax. But they often leave transformed beyond anything they hoped to accomplish in the first place … None of these 'results' was predictable. But they all grew directly out of the meditation [mindfulness] practice.

> Jon Kabat-Zinn

The popularity of mindfulness is growing at an increasingly rapid rate and it is fairly difficult not to hear about it these days. In the UK, the Mindfulness All-Party Parliamentary Group (MAPPG) was launched in Parliament in 2014, supported by the policy institute, The Mindfulness Initiative, which assisted in carrying out an inquiry into how mindfulness could be incorporated into UK services and institutions. In 2015, The Mindful Nation UK Report was launched in Parliament, which is the first evidenced-based policy of its kind seeking to address mental health concerns in areas such as education, healthcare, work and the criminal justice system.

The initiative to incorporate mindfulness into UK services and institutions continues. As of January 2017, 145 British MPs and peers and 250 members of parliamentary staff had completed an eight-week mindfulness course in Westminster.

In October 2017, the UK hosted the world's first summit on mindful politics. Ministers and politicians from no less than 15 countries came together at the House of Commons with the intention to explore how mindfulness might help to reset the conduct of national and international politics. Mindfulness training was proposed to help political leaders to remain resilient, clearheaded and creative in the face of constant change. Increased awareness and compassion amongst politicians might help them to refrain from knee-jerk reactions and give more considered responses, and enable them to make political decisions from a position of balance and equilibrium - decisions that could not only benefit their own countries, but the world as a whole.

So, what is all the hype about? Well, it is difficult not to recognise the multitude of benefits that mindfulness practice can bring when the scientific evidence supporting these is so strong.

Scientifically supported

Over the past few decades, more and more scientific research has been conducted to investigate the effects of mindfulness practice on our brains, minds, emotions, behaviours, functioning and bodies. This research is showing us how mindfulness is effective in the management of many difficulties such as depression, anxiety, stress, psychosis, body image problems, abuse, trauma, eating disorders, ADHD, nicotine addiction, attention and memory problems, low self-esteem, work-related stress, psoriasis, acute and chronic pain, relationship problems, parenting teenagers and children, and much more.

We've highlighted some of these research findings below. Its important to mention however that the specific mindfulness intervention being investigated may differ from study to study, in terms of its duration, particular focus and structure. This book draws on many of the ideas and exercises used within these different mindfulness interventions. Many of the busy people whom we have worked with have told us how the practices in this book have had a positive impact on their well-being, stress and sense of busyness.

Memory, attention and self-control ...

Research has shown how mindfulness practice can change areas of the brain associated with improved cognitive functioning and the ability to regulate emotions. In one study, after only 11 hours of mindfulness practice, structural changes were observed in participants' brains around the anterior cingulate cortex, a part of the brain involved in monitoring our focus and self-control. In another study, participants had brain scans before and after an eight-week mindfulness-based stress-reduction programme. Compared to people who had not done the programme, researchers found increases in key areas of the brain associated with learning and memory processes as well as the ability to take on different perspectives. Whether it is remembering the keys on the way to work, ensuring that you remember to pick up the children from school or learning to use a new computer system, research demonstrates the effectiveness of using mindfulness to aid these vital brain processes. Mindfulness practice also helps to improve our attention, helping to enhance focus and avoid distractions. This is a welcomed benefit for many of us busy people, improving our efficiency by helping us to remain focused on one task at one time. Whether we are at work or at home, often we are surrounded by an ever-increasing number of mobile devices and other people demanding more and more of our attention These days, it is as if our attention is being fractured into tinier and tinier pieces and mindfulness may provide us with the much-needed help to remain focused and to get stuff done, in a more effective and efficient way.

Stress, depression and anxiety ...

Of course, stress is an inevitable part of our everyday lives, from pressing work deadlines or managing a busy household, and at times we may feel overwhelmed. Mindfulness researchers have shown that people who practise mindfulness experience a reduction in stress-related symptoms and an improvement in the way they respond to stress and manage it. They tend to use more helpful coping strategies when in stressful situations, whether at work or at home, helping them to be more productive with their time. And, even when your stress comes from something as scary as cancer, mindfulness has been shown to help people manage and reduce their stress levels in the face of this effectively, too.

Mindfulness practice supports the development of present moment awareness, which has been shown to help improve peoples' perceived competence in handling stressful daily situations (such as an argument with a colleague or loved one or when making a mistake), based on their values, resulting in improvements in their health and general well-being. This is great news, given that these events can be toxic to our health for days at a time, if we do not handle them effectively. It can also help us with our perspective-taking and communication skills more generally, and as already mentioned it can help us to hold back from knee-jerk negative reactions, improving our social connectedness and relationships, which are crucial for human survival and our general well-being.

For people diagnosed with mood disorders, such as depression or anxiety, they are able to tolerate their distress more effectively and become more self-compassionate through training in mindfulness. The Government's National Institute for Clinical Health and Excellence (NICE) continues to recommend that a mindfulness-based cognitive therapy (MBCT) be used for people with recurring episodes of depression. This is unsurprising, considering the results of one study that showed how MBCT was as effective as antidepressant medication in reducing reoccurrence of depression. In another study, which investigated the effects of a mindfulness-based course for 273 people, it was found that in one month following the course there was a 58 per cent reduction in anxiety and a 40 per cent reduction in stress.

Managing our fear response ...

So, why do we experience improved well-being after being 'mindful'? Well, further neurobiological changes within the brain may provide this explanation. Using brain imaging techniques, neuroscientists have observed changes in the 'threat system' of the brain following mindfulness practice. Studies have found that an eight-week mindfulness course reduces the reactivity and the density of neurons in the amygdala (the part of the brain associated with the 'fight or flight response' that triggers fear) and increases activity in areas of the prefrontal cortex that help regulate emotions, subsequently reducing stress.

Other research into the brain's electrical signals has shown that ongoing mindfulness practice was associated with increased alpha wave activity, linked to relaxation and decreased anxiety. Using brain scan technology, scientists have also shown that other structural changes occur in the brain after mindfulness practice, with more connections between different areas of the brain and an increase in a protective nerve tissue called myelin, essential for healthy brain function. When we use mindfulness to help us to manage our moods and stress levels, observable changes are happening in the brain:

> Changes in brain structure may underlie some of these reported improvements and that people are not just feeling better because they are spending time relaxing.
>
> **Sara Lazar, PhD, of the MGH Psychiatric Neuroimaging Research Programme**

Addiction and healthy eating ...

Mindfulness can also be extremely beneficial for addictions. Mindfulness practice via a relapse prevention group has been shown to help people with addictions to manage their cravings more skilfully so that they were less likely to drink alcohol and use drugs. Similarly, mindfulness practice helps people to remain abstinent from cigarette smoking and has been shown to be five times more effective than a standard smoking cessation programme. A growing body of research is also showing how mindfulness can help people manage eating disorders and how it can assist with general weight management, dieting and losing weight. Mindful eating can help people to make heathier choices around what food they eat and manage the urges and impulses to eat more even when they may already be full.

Physical health, pain and ageing ...

Not only does the use of mindfulness have benefits for our mental health and minds, but there has also been growing evidence supporting the use of mindfulness for improved immune system functioning and better physical health. Illness is something we all try to avoid and mindfulness may help you do just that. Research has shown that, even after eight weeks of mindfulness practice, people had changes in immune functioning with a greater antibody count. Mindfulness practice can also help you manage pain more effectively without the aid of painkillers. After a period of mindfulness practice, participants in research studies report lower pain intensity experiences, both in the laboratory and in real-life chronic conditions such as arthritis and back and neck pain. Research has shown decreased activity in areas of the brain involved in registering pain and increased activity in areas involved in regulating pain. Mindfulness may also be your best anti-ageing secret. Brain imaging has shown that mindfulness practice leads to an increase in grey matter in cortical regions of the brain associated with sensory, cognitive and emotional processing and slows down age-related thinning of the cortex. Further research has shown that people who practise mindfulness over a long period of time, by the time they reach their fifties, their brains appear 7.5 years younger than people who have not been practising.

As we have said, it is not just in health and clinical settings that mindfulness has been proven extraordinarily advantageous and profitable. It has also proven helpful with general sleep problems and can also dramatically improve focus, attention, concentration, creativity and performance in business, sports and exercise, as well as bringing more satisfaction to many areas of our daily activities, such as work and our relationships with friends, colleagues and loved ones.

How beautiful to have something so simple that can bring so much benefit and relief to our lives and to the lives of those around us.

Mindfulness is NOT ...

Before you get cracking, we wanted to quickly dispel some common untruths and myths about mindfulness. The following explanations are designed to get straight to the point, so do not worry if anything feels unclear at this stage. It will all be covered and explained further as you continue reading and start to practise yourself.

... meditation

Contrary to popular assumptions and belief, mindfulness does *not* have to be practised as a formal meditation. Although highly effective, meditation is simply a way to practise, cultivate and reinforce the principles of mindfulness as one way of being, which is all about an increased awareness of your present moment experience; an acceptance towards yourself and your experience and the world around you. We promise you will not have to sit crossed-legged in the lotus position or chant to monotone sounds for hours on end to practise or benefit from mindfulness, unless you want to. We want to show you how you can incorporate mindfulness into your busy life, while you are on-the-go.

... subject to time constraints

Many of our busy clients often tell us that they simply do not have the time to practise mindfulness. Well, they have since discovered, as you will too, that nothing could be further from the truth and this is exactly what this book is all about! Mindfulness is abundant and infinite; it is there with you in every moment in which you live, and it is with you right now as you read the pages of this book. There is ample time and opportunity to practise mindfulness in any moment of your life. It is often best practised during activities that you would usually do habitually, on autopilot mode – such as checking and sending emails on your phone, getting dressed, brushing your teeth, taking a shower, standing in a queue, waiting for a train – so we are certain that you will have lots of opportunities to practise.

... dependent on surroundings

As we have already said, people often say that they are too busy, have too much going on or are surrounded by too many noisy and demanding people, either in the office or at home, for them to take themselves away to find a quiet place to practise mindfulness. It may surprise you to know that we have a lot to be mindful of while surrounded by our noisy or demanding environments. We are going to show you how much opportunity you have to be able to practise mindfulness amidst your busy and stressful life just as it is.

... relaxation

Although mindfulness practice may bring a deeper sense of relaxation and calmness (along with other improvements to your levels of functioning, performing, productivity and creativity in general), it is very important to remember that all these are simply fortunate and welcomed by-products of practising mindfulness. Relaxation and the other improvements listed above are not the goal of mindfulness practice (they may arise as an outcome, especially when we lessen our preoccupation with them); the aim is to cultivate a present moment awareness, a new perspective and a new way of carrying yourself through your busy life.

... losing control, escaping reality, going into a trance, becoming complacent and navel-gazing

This is a very common early misconception that we hear often from our busy clients. In fact, mindfulness is the complete opposite of this assumption. Mindfulness is all about facing reality head-on and becoming more connected with your life experience. With practice, you will become more attuned to yourself and the world around you. You will be more conscious to the changeability of your emotions and you will start to understand yourself with accuracy and clarity, feeling more in control of yourself and your actions. An array of alternative options and ideas will then open up for you, for you to choose to move on, ensuring that you have the best opportunity to act in your interest and move towards what truly matters to you in any context of your life.

... selfish, lazy and a waste of time

Many of us feel that we would be selfish or lazy if we spent time on practices for self-development. We believe that we simply cannot look after ourselves until everyone else and everything else is attended to first. Well, again, nothing could be further from the truth on both accounts.

First, mindfulness takes effort and a lot of discipline (there is nothing lazy about it) – it is about cultivating the most profound paradigm shift in our way of being that is known to mankind, and that certainly is not easy. Years of reinforced habits, which may not be serving us so well, are being observed with each practice, while new, and possibly more helpful, habits are being established at the same time.

Second, and further to all this, if we believe that we cannot take time out for ourselves to help us cope better and de-stress until everything else is attended to first (which will never actually be achieved), then it would be fair to say that we run the risk of burnout, leaving us totally immobilised to give any more of ourselves, our time, our attention and our energy to others and the work and relationships that we consider important to us.

Selfishness and laziness (should they arise for you) are both experiences to be observed within mindfulness practice and the very act of observing them leaves us with the choice of whether or not we want to act on them.

... clearing your mind of thoughts

This is a common incorrect assumption that captures the very essence of what mindfulness is all about. Mindfulness is about noticing and being open to all our experiences, including our thoughts. There is no agenda of clearing thoughts from your mind, but just awareness of what thoughts are present in your mind at any given moment. If you try to clear your mind of thoughts, you will soon know about it because you will become frustrated immediately – it is impossible! Distraction by our thoughts is inevitable within mindfulness practice and not a sign of failure. Each distraction is another opportunity to cultivate present moment awareness (mindfulness). Once you've noticed that you are distracted, you can congratulate yourself, as that's what mindfulness is.

... a quick fix to all my problems

Practising mindfulness is by no means a guarantee to get rid of or fix all the undesirable experiences in your life (if that were possible, we promise we would definitely be writing about that now instead). It is more a technique for understanding these as part of the ever-changing 'weather' of our experiences, and that it is often the very resistance to what we perceive as problems or problematic emotions that cause us greater suffering, and may even prolong them.

Mindfulness is to be cultivated and grown as a way of being, over time – there is no agenda (apart from cultivating more awareness of your experience) and no end goal. The very practice of mindfulness may bring with it frustration, disappointment, discouragement, stress, despondence and even anxiety. It is all about bringing an awareness and an acceptance to our experience and with that you are more likely to experience less frequent and intense episodes of undesirable feelings, simply as a welcomed by-product.

Mindfulness is easy to start

The beauty is that you can incorporate mindfulness into your everyday activities. Now, this does not mean that you can carry on aimlessly about your busyness and benefit from all that mindfulness has to offer you. You will have to bring a *purposeful intention of openness and curiosity* to your everyday experiences, to incorporate mindfulness into whatever you may be doing. Are you willing to give it a go? In doing so, we assure you that these mundane, everyday tasks might never feel the same again. Your eyes will open with amazement to the beauty of your life unfolding; you will notice what you have never noticed before and take more enjoyment from things that you thought would be impossible to enjoy.

Mindfulness top tips to-go

In this chapter, you have learned the following:

▶ Mindfulness is scientifically proven to have benefits for a wide range of common difficulties.

▶ There are many unhelpful 'myths' that get in the way of practising mindfulness.

▶ A purposeful effort is necessary to practise mindfulness.

▶ Mindfulness can dramatically improve your busy life.

Understanding how to be mindful

Let us now take a look at what is involved in practising mindfulness. The good news is that what you do in your life might not need to change at all. Nothing external to your mind needs be any different: no person, situation or environment, or even thoughts about these, needs to change. In fact, you can carry on being as busy as you are, yet how you experience your life can become radically different. This may sound like a paradox, but think optical illusions, play on words or those funny conversations that leave you at cross purposes and you may begin to grasp that it is our mind that has the power to create these shifts in perception and, with mindfulness, we can start to learn to do this intentionally. This is a very ancient concept in mindfulness and Eastern spiritual practices:

> Two similar objects appear different because of the difference in the mind that perceives them
>
> **Patanjali, Yoga sutras, 2nd century BCE, verse 15, 'Enlightenment', in translation by Centre for Inner Peace**

You will have experienced the beauty of mindful awareness numerous times in your life, probably as you go about most days, whatever age you are, whoever you are and whatever you get up to. You do not have to acquire it or get it in some way; it is with you already (and right here and now as you read this book), you have always had it and the ability to experience it, you may just want to understand it some more, and develop the skills to reinforce and cultivate more of it.

'Mindfulness' is just a word that is used to attempt to translate a particular way of attending to our experience. Other terms that may feel a little more familiar or palatable that encapsulate and could be used interchangeably with the term mindfulness are: *awareness, consciousness, acknowledgement, observation* or *attention*. Mindfulness is a way of being rather than an object or thing that you attain and so it is even better understood and described as *noticing, knowing, observing, paying attention*, in a particular way.

Mindfulness is all about showing up to your life, turning the lights up on the stage of your rich life experience to illuminate all that is going on for your observation and enjoyment – lap it all up, it is all yours for the taking (good and bad). It is all about bringing awareness to your experience in a purposeful and particular way, with open curiosity and acceptance, without judgement and defence. Most people have described such an experience when listening to music or sitting in a serene setting, say on a beach watching the sunset. Others have described it while playing games and make-believe with their children (in fact, the way children demand our attention makes them excellent mindfulness teachers).

In all these scenarios, it may be that you have become fully immersed and engaged in your experience of the present moment, allowing events to naturally unfold moment to moment as you observe and take it all in, even losing track of time as you do so and somehow all your cares and worries seem far away. The truth is that the clock is still ticking away and any worries that you may have are still there in the background somewhere, but your current activity or surroundings have totally captivated your attention as you observe with curiosity and acceptance. Just think back to the happiest and/or most productive and meaningful moments of your life – we bet there were moments when you were being mindful. The present moment really is a beautiful place to be and we are going to show you how you can spend more time there whenever you choose to.

Focus your attention, here and now!

The good news is that we do not have to wait until we are suddenly drawn into being mindful because our life circumstances have changed (oh, yes, I will be mindful when the sunset attracts my attention) or for a time when we are in the right mood. No, we can be mindful, irrespective of the changing world around us or the ever-changing feelings and thoughts that arise within us. It is all about *you* focusing your attention in a particular way (on purpose, with openness), zooming in on your present moment experience, wherever you are, whatever you may be doing (the choice is yours in any given moment).

Mindfulness practices take many forms but, essentially, all of them share elements of cultivating a disciplined development of awareness – seeing and experiencing the moment just how it is, without attachment or defence. Chögyam Trungpa, a Tibetan Buddhist monk and scholar, wrote of mindfulness:

> Mindfulness is like a microscope; it is neither an offensive nor defensive weapon in relation to the germs we observe through it. The function of the microscope is just to clearly present what is there. Mindfulness need not refer to the past or the future; it is fully now …

The essence of mindfulness has been described by Teasdale (a mindfulness researcher) and his colleagues as a state of being:

> Fully present in the moment, without judging or evaluating it, without reflecting backwards on memories, without looking forward to anticipate the future … and without attempting to 'problem-solve' or otherwise avoid any unpleasant aspects of the present situation

It is time to wake up!

At the centre of mindfulness is acceptance and an open curiosity towards yourself and the world around you; it is not about changing yourself but about noticing what your experience is in any given moment.

Your mind is an expansive space and you may be surprised to know that your thoughts are not the only part of your mind – you have another part of your mind called 'awareness', your *observing mind*, and this part does not produce thoughts, opinions or judgements, it just simply notices and acknowledges *what is* and *how it is*, including the very process of thinking itself. It is the part of you that *knows* and is *aware* that you are thinking; *it is you*. After all, if you can observe your thoughts and notice the process of thinking in your mind, then you cannot also be your thoughts or this thinking.

Your awareness is much like the sky, while your thoughts and emotions are akin to the clouds and weather that pass through the sky. It is helpful to remember that the sky is never overwhelmed by even the fiercest weather conditions, it always has enough room for even the strongest storms or ferocious hurricanes. Just like the sky, your awareness is never overwhelmed by the strongest emotions or the most troublesome thoughts; it has space for them all. It might also be helpful to remember that, sooner or later, the weather always changes.

Understandably, our brains have increased in size over the centuries from those of our primeval ancestors and, as you may know, we are now classified as Homo sapiens sapiens, which, quite basically, translates to: *Man (or woman) who is aware and is aware that s/he is aware*. Amazing, isn't it? The sad thing is that we hardly ever use our awareness. We have the ability to be self-aware but we spend most of our time rushing around, gobbling down food, grabbing at what we want and running from what we do not like, acting on impulse, instinctively without much awareness at all, a bit like our cave-dwelling ancestors did. This way of being can, of course, be helpful and it has its uses at times, but often it can also get us into trouble. In practice, how often do we actually use this awareness part of our mind?

Before you read on we ask that you take 10 seconds now to try the following exercise, which will help you to notice the difference between your thinking mind (thoughts) and your 'awareness' mind. Yes, 10 seconds (you read that right), that is all it takes!

Practice 2.1: Mindfulness right now!

Just 10 (seconds)

▶ When you have read through these simple instructions, close your eyes for the next ten seconds and try to notice and acknowledge the sensation in your body where your body makes contact with the surface on which you are sitting, laying or standing – this may be the sensation on your bottom or back where either meets the chair or bed, or the sensation on the soles of your feet where they meet the floor or the inside of your shoes.

▶ Simply notice and acknowledge this sensation, in other words hold it in your awareness, focus your attention on it and allow it to take centre stage at the forefront of your mind – nothing more than that. Not so much thinking about it, but curiously exploring, and noticing the feeling and the sense of touch of your body making contact with the surface.

▶ Should any thoughts pop into your mind about the exercise, any judgements or opinions about it or anything else at all (maybe about your body or what you need to get done generally), just notice these thoughts, do not try to push them away and gently bring your attention back to noticing and focusing on the sensation in your body.

▶ Just rest in awareness while you notice and concentrate on this sensation for ten seconds right now before reading on. Do not count the seconds, just take a rough guess of how long to do the exercise for, during which try to pay full attention, being as curious as you can be, to the sensation in your body described above.

▶ As we said, it might help to close your eyes.

What did you notice? Did you notice the sensation in your body or thoughts in your mind or both? Most people report how they become more aware of their 'awareness' when doing this exercise and certainly about noticing the difference between being in 'awareness' versus being in their thinking mind. Do not worry if you were not able to stay in your awareness mind for the whole ten seconds; that was not the goal anyway. It is more like a dance, our attention moving in and out of awareness, sometimes our thinking mind is taking the lead and at other times it is our awareness that leads. Noticing where your attention is, is being mindful. Just like a professional dancer or an athlete who both train to stay at the top of their game, we all need to train the mind to focus our attention and be more aware, and this takes practice.

It is also common for people to describe how they felt relaxed or a sense of stillness or peace when dropping into awareness. The reason for this is that there are no thoughts in our 'awareness', and therefore there is no cause of stress. Being in awareness versus your thinking mind is to experience the most classic definition of the term *human being* (rather than *human doing*); we are simply just *being,* being present in our experience right now, rather than *doing* (or *thinking*) anything about it.

Despite all this, it is important to remember that dropping into awareness (or truly noticing your experience in any given moment and in this instance a sensation in our body) is not a relaxation exercise (relaxation is just a fortunate by-product) but first and foremost an exercise of the mind. At first, it may feel a little strange to be in awareness, to be still feels unusual or uncomfortable for so many of us, as if there is something not right or weird about stillness, self-reflection or just *being* and *not doing.* If you felt odd, do not worry, this is totally normal, we are so used to *doing* and rushing around it is understandable if this feels strange to begin with. If you did not notice any of the above, put your book down and try the exercise again before you read any more.

A Mindful Attitude

(adapted from Kabat-Zinn, 2004)

When starting out in the practice of mindfulness it can be helpful to cultivate the following states of mind to help you further reap the benefits.

➤

Non-judging – the mind is constantly judging. We can learn to bring a non-judgment to these judgments by noticing them with curiosity and returning to the focus of your attention. Simply being with whatever arises.

Patience – the mind is keen to move onto the next moment. We can develop a skill of returning to this moment.

Beginner's mind – Be curious and playful, treating each practice and each moment as a possibility for new sensations and experiences.

Trust – Freeing yourself up from the mind's harshness and opening yourself up to your knowledge and intuition.

Non-striving – Letting go of any expectations and attempts to change what is here right now.

Acceptance – bringing kindness and openness to all our experience.

Letting go – not holding on to or pushing away anything that shows up in the mind and body.

And breathe …

Throughout this book and its practices, you will see that we encourage you to notice your breath here and there. Our breath is really a great way to reconnect to ourselves when everything around us is kicking up a storm. The beauty is that our breath is always with us, it is the only certainty that we have in life (apart from our death) as we go about our crazy busy existence. So, if you find you are not breathing, you have probably met with the other certainty and, if you are still breathing, good news … you can practise mindfulness with your breath whenever you like. Our breath continues to go on, without any conscious effort from ourselves, always there, always present, our dear old reliable friend.

Touching base with our breath by focusing our attention on it is often like putting on the brakes when we are going around in circles, or dropping an anchor when a storm has set us off course. Dropping into awareness of our breath is stabilising and reassuring, we can use it to anchor ourselves to this present moment of reality (just as we can with the sensations in our body as we saw above) when it feels like the sh*t has, or is just about to, hit the fan!

Practice 2.2: I haven't got time for this!

The two-minute-breathing space

▶ Close your eyes or rest your gaze on a still object or point in front of you.

▶ Drop into noticing your breath right here, right now.

▶ You do not have to change your breathing or alter it in any way, no need to push or pull on your breath. Your breathing happens naturally, without any need to control it.

▶ Just notice it, as it naturally is, its natural rhythm and sensations.

▶ See if you can notice the sensation of air rise into your nostrils as you breathe in and the sensation of breath leaving your nostrils as you breathe out.

▶ Pay attention to the rise of your stomach as you breathe in and the fall of your stomach as you breathe out.

▶ There it is – your breath, with its natural rhythm and sensations, in this moment.

▶ And then there is you, noticing your breath in this moment.

▶ Remain aware of your breath, ride the waves of your breathing with your full attention.

▶ Follow each in breath from its beginning to its natural end.

▶ Follow each out breath from its beginning to its natural end.

▶ See if you can notice and acknowledge the pause at the end of each in breath before it loops to turn into the next out breath.

▶ See if you can notice the pause at the end of each out breath before it loops back to turn into the next new in breath.

▶ Allow your breath to take centre stage in your awareness right now.

▶ No matter how many times your attention may wander from your breath (remember this is normal and what human minds do), you may be distracted by thoughts, sounds, feelings or sensations, just notice the distraction, congratulate yourself for noticing it, and gently guide your attention back to noticing your breathing. Returning to the sensations and rhythm of your breathing, again and again.

▶ Just this one breath, just this one moment, right here and right now. Notice how each breath is unique.

▶ Allow your breathing, as it is, with its sensations and rhythm to take centre stage in your awareness.

▶ After a few more mindful breaths, gently open your eyes and notice and acknowledge a few objects around you with the same present moment awareness, see if you can continue to drop into awareness using your breath as a focal point, throughout your day.

So, how was that? Not so bad, we assume. If it was, then what did you notice and what was difficult? Was it annoying, frustrating, was it difficult to focus your attention? What expectations or thoughts were getting in the way? Did you try too hard to get it right? Mindfulness is a discipline; it is simple but not always so easy. If you noticed it was hard to focus on the breath because your mind kept wandering off, then well done, great noticing! The mind is designed in a way that makes it unruly and highly conditioned and that means it is hard to stay focused. This is quite natural, it is not 'wrong' for the mind to wander or to have persistent thoughts or images. Sometimes this is very useful to us (for example for planning), and mindfulness is not about trying to stop or prevent this happening, rather it is a great way of highlighting all this, our habitual tendencies and struggles. Hold onto that point for now, we are going to come back to it soon enough.

What is your purpose?

It might be useful at this point to take a moment to reflect on your personal intentions for incorporating mindfulness practice in to your busy life. Although there is no goal to mindfulness practice, it can be helpful to consider what matters most to us when practising mindfulness. Give it a go right now, and you can continue to reflect on this over the course of your mindfulness practice also.

Practice 2.3: Mindfulness right now!

Mindful intentions

Allow the following questions to drop in to your awareness, without trying to think about them too much. Grab something to write on and jot down your answers as they show up.

▶ Mindfulness practice will help me …

▶ I choose to practise mindfulness because …

▶ I hope that mindfulness will change …

▶ If I practise mindfulness, then I will …

▶ To me, mindfulness means …

So, what came up for you? Perhaps you hope to be more able to manage your stress, be more relaxed, improve your performance at work, have better relationships, have more fun, feel more energised. Mindfulness can help with all of these things and many more, so do come back to these questions when you find your motivation wanes. Also, remember that waning motivation can be observed mindfully and it is OK for your enthusiasm to ebb and flow, you do not need to give yourself a hard time if your relationship to practising changes. You might like to just (mindfully) observe any habitual thought patterns you have that may feel aversive and demotivating and then review the questions above in a fresh light.

Mindfulness top tips to-go

In this chapter, you have learned the following:

▶ You do not need to change your life or any of its circumstances to practise and benefit from mindfulness.

▶ Mindfulness is something that you already have and are familiar with.

▶ Mindfulness cultivates a part of our mind called 'awareness'.

▶ Practising 'being aware' is fundamental to mindfulness.

▶ Becoming aware of your breathing can help you reconnect and make contact with the present moment when you feel stressed and busy.

▶ Connecting with your inner intentions can help motivate you in your mindfulness practice.

3

Chasing a stress-free existence

Let us accept it, as there really is no getting away from it; we live in a busy, frantic and stressful world. Not only are we bombarded by daily and even 'moment-to-moment' demands on our time and attention, but also we are obsessed with the pursuit of happiness and high achievement, risking dangerous stress levels, meltdown or much worse.

The truth is that busyness and stress are inevitable parts of our lives, especially when living in these modern times amidst ever-increasing advancements in technology and more and more pressure to perform at peak levels in all areas of life, all around the clock! There seems to be a great paradox that has arisen in our modern society. The more we invent smarter and faster ways of getting things done, the more we are creating a frightening world of information overload and are also caging ourselves in increasing levels of stress (that we just want to escape from most of the time).

We are overwhelmed by daily demands and pressures, shooting off emails here and there, checking and updating our increasing collection of social media, ensuring that we are kept in the loop while also not ignoring others, working harder and longer to keep our jobs during unpredictable times, including when we are not even physically present in the office, helping friends, family and the postman's cat with all manner of problems, and generally spending much of our time rushing from one task to the next, trying to get everything done, attended to and ticked off of our to-do list. Phew! That was a lot to get condensed in one sentence and there surely is even more to get done in reality.

Now, on top of that daily grind, there are still the inevitable traumatic incidents and derailing upheavals to deal with that life throws at us from time to time. These events tend to come without much warning, out of the blue and unexpected, and many of them can prove to be life-changing and challenging to cope with, such as the illness or death of a loved one, an acute or chronic physical injury or illness of our own, a relationship ending, a sudden redundancy or even a car theft, to name just a few common possibilities.

In the absence of such eventualities, we seem to forget to leave any room for them as we go about our daily routines and meeting all the demands we face, filling up our days – which are often already bursting at the seams – with more and more stuff. It is as if most of us are walking along a very fine tightrope indeed, about to lose our balance with the next unforeseen pressure flying at us from any angle out of the blue, and then we fall, crashing to the ground. Sound familiar?

As if all this was not enough to contend with, along the way we also seem preoccupied with achievement and securing success in nearly all aspects of

life while also searching for some peace, relaxation and happiness via whatever means as if such a time and state could be reached and then maintained indefinitely. The more we strive for this illusion, it is understandable that we will, inevitably, become more stressed, anxious, depressed and burnt out. If we really look at the pressure we put ourselves under and all that we are expected to cope with, it would seem that most of us think we are superhuman and would presume to find ourselves among others in the DC Comics' superheroes' hall of fame.

Practice 3.1: Mindfulness right now!

What busy superhero am I?

See if you can recognise your *busy self* among any of these busy superhero profiles. Once you have read through them, have a think about which you are most like.

Work-O-Holic – saving the world with a spreadsheet!

Work-O-Holic is busy with work, racing against the clock and trying to rid the world of unrelenting workloads, crowded and cluttered email inboxes, general

➤

---

disorganisation, messy and abstract agendas and failing projects. Using certain secret superpowers and tools such as his/her acute and pedantic attention to detail, skilful planning, organisational and procedural prowess and trusty spreadsheets and the invincible power to run millions of to-do lists at once, Work-O-Holic is tirelessly rushing from one work task to the next, zapping piles of paperwork, disorder and the potential for global failure where it really hurts!

Captain Do-Good – saving the world with a cupcake!

Do-Good is busy pleasing others, taking on tasks for everyone that may (or may not!) need some help, trying to rid the world of others' unhappiness and pain. With a steady flow of cupcakes baking in the oven, a spectacular collection of miraculous cleaning products at hand, extra booster seats for the school run and superhuman solutions for all – oh, and a bionic sympathetic listening device to boot – he/she is set to relieve others of discomfort and ensure that they always have someone to rely on forever, come rain or shine! No one will ever feel unwanted or neglected again with Captain Do-Good protecting the planet!

Fantastic Mr Fox – saving the world with a treadmill!

Fantastic Mr Fox is busy with working out in the gym and spinning classes a lot of the time, trying to rid the world of ugliness and physical imperfections. With a rolling gold-plus gym membership, A-list celebrity photos to hand, a full library of bulletproof diets, a trusty plastic surgeon on speed-dial and super-reflective fold-out portable mirrors, Fantastic Mr Fox feels well equipped to win the fight against ageing and ensure global physical perfection once and for all!

Dr Cure-All – saving the world with a blood pressure monitor!

Dr Cure-All is busy checking on health, trying to rid the world of disease and death. With supercharged blood pressure monitors, unbreakable mercury-filled thermometers, batches of super-foods and multi super-vitamins at the ready and a broadband connection faster than the speed of light to ensure a direct link to doctors online, Dr Cure-All is on a single-minded mission to eradicate all death, physical illness, weakness, aches and pains!

Saccharinnia/Saccharissimo – saving the world with a Mills & Boon novel!

Saccharinnia/Saccharissimo is busy radiating sparkling love and honeymoon romance for all to enjoy, trying to rid the world of relationship imperfections and boring, unsatisfying and failed marriages. With a supernatural and invincible perception for a partner's flaws and annoyances, a rolling subscription to *Hello* magazine and the full series of Mills & Boon novels to hand, he/she is relentlessly creating a world where no one ever feels trapped in uncomfortable relationships and tramples on all potential relationship regrets.

Professor Squeeze – saving the world with a jam-packed diary

Professor Squeeze is highly sophisticated at ensuring their diary is full to the brim with activity. Attempting to abolish boredom and time-wasting, Professor Squeeze ensures every minute of the day is productive and worthwhile and has the power to perform several tasks at the same time. Magically requiring almost zero time to recover from the hecticness of the day and sleeping for as little time as possible, allowing more space in the day to complete endless to-do lists and succeed in all areas of life. When a new opportunity arises, Professor Squeeze ensures that they will be there, no matter what. Doing nothing is not an option!

Like most of us, you may have found similarities between bits of yourself and more than one of these busy superheroes (if not, perhaps you would like to make one up for yourself). That is OK and really quite normal; we can all become preoccupied with trying to rid our world of unpleasant scenarios and painful feelings, trying to convince ourselves and/or others that we are somehow invincible! But the point here is that no matter what 'secret superhero powers' you believe you may have to complete your mission, you will never succeed, despite all your best efforts – all you will get is busier, more stressed and unhappier!

The opposite element to these 'super powers' is that underneath we often actually think we are 'failing', not good enough or not fully meeting the expectations of the culture, people, parents, colleagues, etc. around us. This can lead us to think that we are somehow deficient and flawed. Often, this can lead to states of depression and anxiety, attempts to hide our 'true' self or to blame others for our unhappiness. If we are not totally incapacitated by our feelings of failure already, we may just keep steaming on at an ever-increasing intensity to maintain our super-hero disguise and status until we collapse.

The busy delusion

Our superheroes are often under the misconception that, if they just keep up all the busyness, it means that they are, indeed, super. The reality is that the more overloaded the brain is, the more our performance can suffer. Our ability to problem-solve, be creative and innovative, manage difficult emotions, make decisions, be productive is easily impaired when our minds become cluttered and tired.

Have a go at the next exercise to remind yourself of this.

Practice 3.2: Mindfulness right now!

Multitasking farce

As you read the paragraph below, you must count all the times the letter 'e' appears. As you do this, you must be counting and reading simultaneously – you cannot read and then go back and count and you cannot keep a record on a piece of paper – you have to do the counting in your head at the same time as reading the words on the page. In addition, accuracy is very important so, if you lose track or are not 100 per cent sure that you have counted correctly, then you have to start all over again – that will happen at least once!

> Research consistently indicates that approximately 80% of the population experiences violent and upsetting thoughts. These thoughts are most likely due to automatic associations produced by the brain. In other words, there is no reflection on one's character for having a brain, which produces these thoughts. This idea is in stark contrast with a traditional therapeutic notion that the unconscious mind possesses deep-seated evil intentions. Given that intrusive thoughts are common, it would be unreasonable to strive for an absence of these thoughts.

Your answer (go on, write it, we dare you, no one's looking!): _____

How did it go? Bit frustrating maybe? The answer is 52, by the way. Not so easy to focus on two (or more) things at once, is it? So, to be less stressed, less busy and more effective, productive, efficient and focused, forget the multitasking, because it is impossible to be truly effective at doing two things at once and will, invariably, stress you out. See how today, or for an hour, a few minutes even, you get along doing just one thing in the moment. Try it now as you read on, let go of any urges to count letters, check your mobile, tweet, drink coffee, plan world domination or anything else that arises and see if you can allow yourself to *really* do just one thing at a time.

The other thing that our superheroes are not too keen on (possibly even their worst nightmare) is doing nothing at all. But, when we really 'waste time' and do nothing, we find that our brains can really benefit. Have you ever found that your most creative insights show up when you are on holiday, away from the usual busyness? It is also why we all need to invest in a waterproof notepad for the shower to capture all those great ideas our mind comes up with, when we just give it the opportunity to rest.

How is busyness working for you?

So, how is all your busyness working out for you? We are not here to tell you what to do, instead, what we are really keen on doing is to encourage you to notice your own experience and let it guide you. Please try to tune into your own experience to understand whether your busy behaviours and any superhero strategies you use to eradicate your stress and busyness are working for you or not. As you reflect on whether the strategies you use are working for you, we encourage you to consider the following three questions:

▶ Is this strategy effective in helping me to feel less busy and better in the short term?

▶ Is this strategy effective in helping me to feel less busy and better in the longer term?

▶ Are there any other consequences of using this strategy on my wider quality of life?

Have a go at the following exercise to reflect on this. You might like to draw out a table like the one shown to help you along. We have included a few examples from what we have heard others tell us to help get you started.

Practice 3.3: Mindfulness right now!

How is busyness working for me?

What strategies have you tried to be less stressed and busy?	Did it make you feel better?		What consequences did this have on your quality of life?
	In the short term?	In the longer term?	
Working harder and longer hours	*Yes – I felt productive and like I was getting on top of things.*	*No – I felt more tired, stressed and busy by the end of the day.*	*I cancelled seeing friends and I felt so pumped up I found it hard to wind down and sleep that night.*
Making lots of to-do lists	*Yes – I felt like I was in control.*	*No – I felt overwhelmed by the lists and like a failure for not getting through all the items.*	*I never got anything done, felt defeated and stayed in bed for the day so I was even less productive and didn't go to the gym as usual.*
Worrying and problem-solving	*No – I felt anxious.*	*No – I felt stuck and more under-confident.*	*I couldn't concentrate on anything else and so didn't get much work done or take care of my partner. My relationship suffered, I argued with my partner.*

➤

What strategies have you tried to be less stressed and busy?	Did it make you feel better?		What consequences did this have on your quality of life?
	In the short term?	In the longer term?	
Drinking alcohol	*Yes – felt immediately better and relaxed.*	*No – felt tired and hungover the next day.*	*It was costly to my health. I spent money on drink that I didn't have. I was lethargic and couldn't get much done the next day, I didn't feel like seeing my friends, so cancelled my plans.*

You may have noticed a bit of a pattern occurring in the example above and in your own experience. Many of our attempts to eradicate stress and reduce our sense of busyness might work in the short term, but do not work too well for us in the long term and come with their own problems, and they can negatively impact our overall quality of life. Noticing this, by being mindful, helps us to decide whether we want to try something different that is less problematic for us in the longer term.

If you are with us on this, you might also agree that the busy superheroes residing within us often are mistaken, so it can be helpful to try and watch out for them when they are taking charge. We want to share an acronym with you that might help you to remember and look out for times when you might be increasing your sense of busyness and stress and draining all the fun and fulfilment out of your life, irrespective of how much you have to do. This is **BUSY:**

B **Believing and buying into your superhero mission.** Are you spending time thinking through all the thoughts in your mind that tell you how busy you are, how much you have to get done, how you cannot fail or let others or yourself down?

U **Unaware of your busy-causing habits and behaviours.** Are you living life on autopilot, rushing around, remaining oblivious and unaware of what you are doing that really keeps you so busy?

S **Struggling with painful feelings, thoughts, sensations and behaviours.** Are you trying desperately hard to escape and avoid all discomfort and pain? Trying to get everything done and attended to, pleasing others and pursuing the obliteration of stress and discomfort in whatever you do?

Y Yearning for something more or different. Are you spending time in the present moment or are you usually thinking about and looking to the past or the future or expecting the world to be different in some way, to find the answers to all your problems? Do you ever stop to savour the moment you are in (warts and all) or do you try ever so hard to rid your world of its imperfections, wanting and wishing for another better time and place?

How about finally letting go of all this busy superhero facade? Is it really working for you? What does your experience tell you? Can you imagine that, amidst all the busyness and rushing around that you inevitably do, you have the capacity to deal with life's imperfections and all the stress and anxiety that arises in life? It may surprise you to know that you do not have to (nor can you) zap this stress and busyness into oblivion, eradicating all your pain once and for all, as if it were your superhero nemesis.

Mindfulness top tips to-go

In this chapter, you have learned that it is helpful to:

▶ Recognise what busy superhero you may be trying to be.

▶ Notice that you may be creating more unnecessary busyness for yourself.

▶ Notice that all this busyness may have some costs and be taking you away from other aspects of your life that you care about.

▶ Try to stop doing everything at once, as multitasking just stresses you out even more and makes you less effective and maybe even give yourself time to do nothing at all.

Tracking your practice

We encourage you to keep a track of your mindfulness practice. So, here, we have provided a summary list of the mindfulness practices that we have covered in Part 1. We would recommend that you continue to practise these and incorporate them into your daily routine as much as you can. To begin with, find a time when life feels a little easier, perhaps when you wake up before getting out of bed, when you are winding down in the evening before you go to bed or when you sit down to eat your lunch, before automatically tucking in to it. You may find that there is no stress or busyness in that very moment, just clarity, resting in awareness of your breath.

You might also like to jot down some notes on your experience of doing these practices, for example, how you found doing them. Were they helpful? What got in the way? What difference did they make to your usual day-to-day experience?

Practice	Page	When?	Notes
2.1: Just 10 (seconds)	17	Throughout the day, e.g. when you go to sit down, travelling on the train to work, lying in bed.	
2.2: The two-minute breathing space	20	Twice a day, perhaps at the start and end of the day, any time during the day when you might feel busy and stressed.	
2.3: Mindful intentions	21	Once or twice in the week or when you find yourself distancing yourself from practice, reflect on your intentions to practise mindfulness.	
3.1: What busy superhero am I?	25	Throughout the day, try to notice when your superhero is in charge.	

Part

2

The mind, stress and mindfulness

Now that we have introduced the basic principles of mindfulness and high-lighted the ways in which it can help you with your busy life, and demonstrated how to start to practise it, we are now keen to turn your attention to *busyness* and *stress* because, let us face it, busyness would not be a problem at all if it felt nice and was not stressful, would it? In this second part of the book we are going to turn your attention to:

▶ What exactly it is that creates more busyness and stress for us.

▶ How we can create more time without changing a thing around us or any of our life circumstances.

▶ Why and how we became such busy creatures.

▶ What happens when we start to feel stressed and what we can do to feel less stressed.

▶ Look at the busy world that goes on in our mind: our thoughts.

▶ Practise lots of mindfulness.

There is no time to waste

Just take a moment right now and consider how much time you really spend analysing your life, trying to think through all that is going wrong, problem-solving, daydreaming about how you would like things to be, planning and plotting your next move to bring about your everlasting happiness and peace. How many of your fantasies are secretly based on and driven by the illusionary belief that, if only things were different, if only you could get all this stuff sorted out, done and dusted, then you would be happy, forever? Be honest with yourself, now!

If you are striving for this fantasy, we can assure you that you will find yourself rushing around like a hamster on a wheel indefinitely. Without addressing this preoccupation lurking within our thoughts and behind our actions, we run the risk of exhaustion, burnout, increasing levels of stress and even more busyness.

Engaging in all these types of behaviours, in an attempt to avoid our stress and busyness, is completely understandable. We are not saying for one second that there is something inherently wrong with you if you notice yourself doing them. In fact, we and most of the people we know tend to do them, too. We are just saying that it might be helpful to take a pragmatic view on them and see if they are really working for you. Sure, in the short term, they are effective; fantasising and thinking in these ways and rushing around a lot feels like it helps, right? It probably does to an extent or, simply, you would not do it. However, as we have seen usually, there are costs in the longer term. We can feel even more stressed and busier. Also, as we rush around on autopilot, we are usually missing out on much of our lives.

Practice 4.1: Mindfulness right now!

How connected to your life are you, really?

Consider whether you have experienced any of the following scenarios over the past week as you have been either daydreaming about how your life should be less hectic and/or planning and plotting your next tactical manoeuvre as you work your way through your never-ending to-do lists:

▶ Zoned out of conversations and forgotten what others have said to you.

▶ Arrived at destinations without any idea of how you got there.

▶ Gobbled down breakfast/lunch/dinner on-the-go without ever actually tasting your food.

▶ Paid more attention to your phone/tablet than to your colleagues, friends or family.

▶ Dwelt on the past or worried about the future.

▶ Skim-read pages of this book!

If you have experienced any or all of these scenarios, then it is likely that you have been living on autopilot, been too caught up inside your thoughts and fantasies of how you think your life should be and caused yourself more stress, more busyness and, generally, taken less satisfaction from your life. These kinds of behaviours represent clues that may remind you how often you choose to mindlessly create more busyness and less satisfaction in your life. It is worth taking a few moments to extend the exercise above to ask yourself the questions in the following exercise.

Practice 4.2: Mindfulness right now!

Am I my own worst enemy?

How do you disconnect from your life experience?

▶ Are you constantly caught up in the thoughts whizzing around your mind?

▶ Do you notice the world around you as you rush about your life?

▶ Do you ever stop for a moment for no other reason but to notice how you feel emotionally or physically, or what you might need – such as food, water, care, attention?

How do you avoid and try to get rid of stress and busyness in your life?

▶ Do you try to do more and more in the hope that soon enough everything will be done and dusted and you can kick back, relax and rest?

▶ Do you drink more alcohol, smoke cigarettes or take drugs to feel less stressed, to get out of your head and get rid of painful, stressful feelings?

▶ Do you veg out in front of the TV or withdraw from loved ones to avoid more hassle and stress in your life?

▶ Do you take little care of yourself; eat microwaveable meals or snacks on-the-go, rarely exercise, sleep less, so you have more time for other more 'vital' things?

Are you fearful of failing or being judged by others?

▶ Does this lead you to try to be perfect in everything you do? Do you constantly say 'yes' or immediately respond to all and sundry who ask something of you?

Are you preoccupied with worry and self-critical thoughts?

▶ Does your mind race with stressful thoughts about what you should be doing, what you have not done, maybe how you are not good enough and you should be doing more and better?

Are you engaged with your busy story?

▶ Constantly replaying this script, telling yourself and anyone else who can bear to listen how busy you are, how much you have to get done, how unfair and stressful your life is?

Do you ever stop to really consider what is most important to you in life?

▶ How does 'doing' busy affect your mental and physical health, well-being, vitality, relationships?

▶ How would you like to be remembered when your time is up, how would you like to know that you lived your life – as a busy and stressed person or a caring, connected, efficient, calm, compassionate person, maybe?

Lap it up!

We are so preoccupied with all that we have to get done that, even if we do find we have five minutes to kill here and there, we usually use that time to think through what we should be doing or where we should be next or to replay some past encounter or mishap over and over in our mind or worry about what is coming up. We miss out on so much of our experience this way. What about coffee breaks? How often have you really enjoyed a 'break'?

These mini intervals throughout the day are rarely that, or moments of any form of rest or coffee satisfaction. In fact, often, they are just another habit, full of other mini habits being lived out on autopilot (without much awareness) at the same time. Also, often, we are doing more things at the same time, such as tweeting, getting dressed, reading some paperwork, checking emails, talking to someone, watching TV or listening to the radio. How many times do you really just sit and have a cup of coffee, for no other reason at all than just that?

The purpose of the next exercise is to begin to show you just how you can bring and incorporate mindfulness into your everyday activities (we will be doing much more of this throughout the remainder of the book), such as drinking coffee. It will show you how you have the power to break old habits and live a more meaningful and enjoyable life. This exercise will allow you to start to use your coffee interludes for the reason they were intended – to have a break from the endless rushing around that you do all day long – often inside your head.

If you do not drink coffee, you can try this exercise with any other drink you choose (or even a cigarette, if you smoke – just be aware and curious in the same way as outlined below). If you drink your coffee in public, do not worry about anyone noticing what you are doing, as you drink it mindfully, they will just think that you are deep in thought – which is what most of them will be doing anyway and secretly what you are not doing! Remember, there is no agenda to have any particular experience of drinking your coffee – the only goal is to pay attention to whatever your experience is.

So, go and get a cup of coffee (or whatever your vice may be) and try this exercise out now or as soon as you can.

Practice 4.3: I haven't got time for this!

Wake up and smell the coffee!

▶ First, hold your cup of coffee in both hands (and, if you usually do this, experiment by holding it some other way). Notice the weight of the coffee cup plus the liquid inside it. Notice the heat of the cup against your hands and fingers.

▶ Acknowledge and be aware that you are noticing the weight and the heat of the cup. There is the weight and the heat of the coffee cup and then there is you noticing it. Allow the weight and heat of the coffee cup to take centre stage in your awareness.

▶ Do not worry if you cannot feel the weight or heat enough or properly, remember this is not about the weight and heat, it is about awareness and acceptance of what is, just as it is.

▶ Bring the coffee cup closer to your face and notice the aroma, soaking it up as it fills the space in front of your face.

▶ It is natural for your attention to wander or become distracted. When this happens, just gently guide it back to noticing your coffee and the sensations you experience.

▶ Now, as you bring the cup closer to your mouth in anticipation of the first sip, notice the movement in your body, hands and lips.

▶ Acknowledge the fact and be aware that you are noticing the movement in your body, hands and lips. There is the movement in your body, hands and lips and then there is you noticing this movement. Allow the movement in your body, hands and lips to take centre stage in your awareness.

▶ Now, as you take a sip of coffee, notice the temperature of the warm liquid enter your mouth and any physical responses in your body.

▶ Notice and experience the taste of the coffee.

▶ Be aware that you are noticing the taste of the coffee.

▶ Before you swallow, notice the natural impulse to swallow. Once you have swallowed, acknowledge how your body is now one sip of coffee heavier.

▶ Now, notice the gap of time after you have swallowed before you take the next sip of coffee into your mouth.

▶ Your experiences of drinking coffee change – but the part of you that notices all these experiences does not change, it remains simply aware, nothing more, nothing less.

▶ Should your attention wander or become distracted, just gently guide it back to noticing your coffee and any sensation that you experience.

Busy, tricky minds

The truth is that there is nothing else to blame for our busyness, no one else, no endless emails, no after-school activities, no relentless work projects, no annoying friends, uncaring partners, demanding bosses or slack colleagues – in fact, nothing else at all is responsible for our escalating stress levels, frantic rushing, gruesome schedules and general busyness, except our busy thinking minds! Now, that does not mean that you are to blame, that you are at fault or that there is something fundamentally wrong with you or your mind. This is just how our minds have evolved and they are doing just what they are designed to do (more on this later in this chapter). However, we can do something about all this. We can take responsibility for managing our minds and choose how we respond to them when they are busy, keeping us busy. Try making a list or having a think right now of all the things that you assume make you more stressed and busier in life. We have listed a few of our own recurring rants to help you get started.

Practice 4.4: Mindfulness right now!

What slows you down and makes you stressed and busier?

▶ Waiting in queues.

▶ Moving through a crowd on the tube.

▶ Traffic jams/roadwork delays.

▶ Losing my phone/no internet connection.

▶ Too many emails!

▶ Others taking ages to make their point.

▶ *My mind!*

What if, the next time you are in a situation such as the ones listed above (or any others that you came up with), that, instead of becoming caught up in thoughts about how everything is in your way, how delayed and slowed down you are, what you have to do next, how you will not be able to get everything done, fantasising how your life should be versus how you are experiencing it in that moment and generally being caught up in all the frustration that arises with this, that you actually just become aware of this fantasy-fuelled story, nothing more and nothing less than that.

Just notice who or what exactly is making you more stressed out and increasing your sense of busyness in that very moment – is it the situation and people around you, the buzz of the endless message alerts going off on your phone or *your mind* and all the worrying and frustration-fuelled ranting that it is *doing* about the situation? Sure, the demanding situations that we find ourselves in can stress us out and keep us busy, yet all this usually is made worse by us buying into all the stressful thoughts produced by our minds.

Time is ticking away!

As we rush around amidst our busyness, all too often it seems as if there simply is not enough time in the day to get everything done. However, time simply ticks away at the same pace for everyone, every day, whether it feels like it is going faster or not. The reason that on some days it seems to whizz past us faster than the speed of light is often all down to our worry about it slipping away, our worry that there just never is enough time in the day. While we are worrying in this way, we are simply not present or 'awake' enough to experience real time at all. Take Sandra in the following case example, for instance. She worried that she had no time for herself (and it is fair to say, like the rest of us, she had a lot on and to take care of) but, in all her worry about this, she missed the point that she had lots of time for herself – the same amount of time that we all have.

Sandra

When Sandra came to therapy, she was in tears and she looked exhausted. She was busy, busy, busy – dividing her time between her husband, her three children, her work and her friends. She explained that she was working hard not to leave anyone out and she planned her days carefully so that she gave everyone and everything the time that she felt they deserved – the sad fact was that she never felt that she had any time left for herself. She fantasised about taking long hot baths, getting her hair done, doing some shopping, curling up on the sofa with her book. But, the more she fantasised about all this, the more it upset her and the more she felt increasingly busier and as if there was never enough time in the day for her.

The reality was that Sandra was just too preoccupied with time and how she did not have enough of it – sure, her life was busy and demanding but, even in the face of this fact, she had ample time for herself and she just did not see it; she spent most of it worrying that she never had it! Her time was not restricted in any way at all, it was, in fact, abundant just as it is for all of us, no matter how busy we are. Sandra was waiting for a time when there were no demands on her to take time for herself. The truth is that, in every moment – whether she was spending time with others or not – she always had the possibility to spend time with herself also.

All time is *my time*!

When our life is so busy, we feel the need to allocate time to tasks, which can, of course, be helpful, but we must try to remember that all this time is, in fact, *our* time. It is only when we are wanting something different from right now that we are not having any *me* time. You can learn to bring awareness to your everyday experiences with mindfulness and, inasmuch, feel that you have ample and unlimited time to spend with yourself. Everywhere you are, everywhere you go, whatever you are doing and whomever you are with – surprise, surprise, you are also there, experiencing life just as it is! As you go about your everyday busy routine, make a conscious effort to check in with your experience of that moment – you might run through a quick list of short questions as outlined in the following exercise, to silently answer to yourself that will help you to feel present, taken care of (by yourself!) and attended to.

Practice 4.5: I haven't got time for this!

Spending time with yourself wherever you are

▶ How am I feeling right now?

▶ How am I standing, walking, sitting right now?

▶ How does my body feel right now?

▶ What am I doing right now?

▶ What thoughts are being produced by my mind right now?

▶ Is buying into these thoughts or acting in this way helping me live a productive and meaningful life?

▶ What do I *really* need in this moment?

▶ What is really important to me right now?

▶ How would I like to be in this moment?

▶ What do I want to stand for in the face of this situation I am in?

Letting time slip away

Keeping a track of time does not interfere with being present in any given moment or the practice of mindfulness whatsoever, please do be assured of that. That said, time itself and our relationship to it are entirely part of our constructions of the world, they are no more 'real' than days of the week, months or years. Time is simply a useful construct to help orient ourselves and coordinate ourselves with others. Just like any event in the world, we can make various meanings from this and judge ourselves and others in relation to these. Being 'punctual', 'rushing', 'late', 'slovenly' or 'lazy' usually all entail some concept of time, as do many other ideas of our identity, such as our time in history, age and sense of achievement or milestones.

Sometimes, it is helpful to reflect on how time serves us in these ways, or whether it can feed into habitual patterns of our *thinking* mind (more of this to come) that take us away from the present and away from the moment we are in. This can give us an overwhelming sense of time slipping away further, adding to a sense of always trying to play catch-up. However, if you bring more present, focused awareness to your experience at any given moment (as outlined in the exercise above), you will find that time does not seem to slip away so often.

One of the best ways to develop a more helpful relationship with time is to practise mindfulness of a watch or clock. A dial watch, rather than a digital watch, is much easier to start to practise with. We do not have to think about it, work the time out or how much more time we may have left to do what we are doing – usually, we visualise and know all this by observing where the hands of the clock are – we just simply *know* the time. By contrast, when we read the time from a digital display, often we start to think about and calculate the time and how much time we have left to do something or get somewhere. If you tend to check the time on your phone, set the time display to a dial (maybe download an app for this) also.

Practice 4.6: I haven't got time for this!

Watching time – tick, tock!

▶ Look at a watch or clock (with a dial display) and check the time now. Know, acknowledge and notice what time it is.

▶ Be aware that you are noticing the time. There is no need to think about or calculate what time it is at all, see it, know it, there it is, the time.

▶ Acknowledge where the hour hand, minute hand and second hand are.

▶ Notice the difference in space between these hands.

▶ Notice the sound, if any, that is coming from the watch or clock.

▶ Notice the silence in between the sounds it makes.

▶ Should any thoughts about what you are doing, the time in general, what time it is or is not, how much time you have left, what a waste of time this is, or any others show up at all, just notice these thoughts, let go of them, congratulate yourself for noticing them, and let them drift by as you bring your attention back to noticing, acknowledging and knowing the time right now, in this moment.

▶ There it is, the time, and then there is you, noticing the time.

▶ Should any feelings show up, any anxiety, boredom or frustration, just acknowledge these feelings, congratulate yourself for acknowledging them, and gently guide your attention back to observing time and knowing the time right now.

▶ There it is, the time, and then there is you, noticing and knowing the time.

▶ Your experiences of watching the time change, your thoughts, feelings about the time come and go, but the you that simply knows, notices and is aware of the time does not change.

▶ There is time and then there is you noticing and knowing the time.

Slowing time down

You may have noticed that, with each passing year, time seems to pass by much more quickly. One explanation for this phenomenon is that the older we get, the fewer new experiences we have and the world becomes more familiar, so less information needs to be wired in to our brains. And, when we want to speed up time, perhaps we are at the dentist, in a boring meeting, taking a long flight to somewhere sunny and relaxing, then we tend to busy our minds with distractions. So, another way to slow down time is by not comparing our current experience with our past or future, not relying on distractions to avoid unpleasant feelings and, instead, to really live in the present.

Making comparisons and narrowing our sense of the world around us (been there, done that, got the T-shirt), decreases our curiosity, our openness to wonder and capacity for new experiences. And, if instead, we choose to increase our opportunity for new experiences, simply by being mindful of the uniqueness of even one breath, or sip of coffee, we can experience time more slowly, too. By replacing old habits with new habits, you can also slow down time, without taking up any time at all. This also allows a sense of spaciousness to emerge within the mind, a new and restful openness to life and a sense that we do, in fact, have time. From this place, we can begin to establish contact with life as it unfolds, in more meaningful, wonderful, less stressful ways.

Practice 4.7: Mindfulness right now!

Changing old habits

Take a look at the following list and see if there are any habits you might like to change. Feel free to come up with your own:

▶ Take a different route to the corner shop or to work.

▶ Try a different brand of tea/coffee.

▶ Watch a new documentary/film rather than your usual TV show.

▶ Go to a new café for lunch.

▶ Try cooking a new recipe for dinner.

▶ Listen to a different style of music.

▶ Make a phone call instead of sending a text.

It all began with a 'busy' caveman

As we rush around frantically and tirelessly, busily pursuing everlasting happiness, we are using the same part of our brain as our cave-dwelling ancestors used when they strove for survival amidst an unfamiliar and threatening world – our flight or fight response.

Sure, unlike cavemen, we may not be running from wild animals today, but we are 'running' towards perfection, success, happiness and relaxation and, simultaneously, we are 'running away' from the opposite (imperfection, failure, unhappiness, *busyness*) – a threat, in the same way that wild animals were to our cavemen ancestors.

Today, striving for complete perfection, relaxation and happiness via our endless attempts at thinking through and analysing our life problems, evaluating our lives and how we would prefer them to be and then acting on the back of all these thoughts, the more our bodies release the same amount of cortisol and adrenalin, our stress hormones, and the more we come to experience the same level of anxiety and stress throughout much of our daily lives as our ancestors did running from wild animals. The less busy we try to become, the busier we are!

In their necessary survival mode, our cave-dwelling ancestors evolved to develop a strong sense of fear to keep them on high alert for the next potential danger. They felt uneasy most of the time, as a result, as they constantly scanned their environment for threats. Most animals, say like a zebra that has been chased by a lion and lived to see another day, quite quickly will be able to go back to its usual calm state once it has reached safety. Our cave-dwelling ancestors, on the other hand, would continue to think about the threat after they had managed to escape the lion's jaws, and probably also continue to think about how and when a similar attack might happen to them again. A great survival tool we are sure you would agree, as all the while they could keep their arousal levels high, ready for fight or flight when needed again.

Our brains today have not evolved much over this time and, in this respect, we continue to be on high alert to the next potential looming problem or danger that may bring about our very own modern-day downfalls. Of course, thankfully, there are fewer physical threats to our survival these days but, nonetheless, we do still inherently scan our present-day, busy lives for potential threats to our survival – and, let us face it, there is still a lot of stuff that poses a threat these days! As we mentioned earlier, there is work to get done, there are jobs to keep, bills to pay, children to get to school and feed, homework and housework to be done, emails to answer, friends and family to keep happy, health and fitness to maintain, etc. Thinking about getting all this done can leave us feeling highly stressed, exhausted and, not to mention, defeated when everything is not ticked off the to-do list at the end of each day.

Our preoccupation with these threats is learned and driven by our attempts to eradicate any feelings of failure and rejection in life – or, in other words, to avoid our modern-day downfall and ensure our survival, just as our ancestors did many years ago. We have learned from our ancient, scatty predecessors that the feelings of failure and rejection are connected to our decline, our ceasing to survive – they are scary and must be avoided at all costs (more of this to come in the next part of this book) so we try anything and everything we can to eradicate or escape from these scary feelings (which is not possible) as much as we can.

The learned survival 'gift' from our ancestors is never asleep and is constantly ticking away in our thoughts in the form of our worrying, reminiscing, problem-solving, analysing, planning and evaluating. It is constantly alert to all that we do not have, all that we have not done, all that might go horribly wrong, all that we cannot cope with due to the way that we feel and others' negative appraisals of us. If we remain unaware of it and our automatic tendency to become caught up in it, then we run the risk of going into overdrive, leading to more stress and physical aches and pains, more inefficiency and all the life discomfort and dissatisfaction that we will, inevitably, come to experience as a result.

Down the stress well

Our experience of stress comes in all shapes and sizes. We experience racing thoughts, painful emotions, uncomfortable bodily sensations and we also find ourselves doing lots of busy behaviours. These experiences are just that, experiences that come and go. What usually happens is that we over-identify with them as if they are us. We might hear ourselves saying stuff like; 'I am stressed' or 'I am exhausted' – well, the truth is that you are neither, you are *you* and you are experiencing stressful feelings in your emotions and sensations of tiredness in your body in that moment – there is a big difference.

With mindful awareness, we can stand back from and give space to our experiences, such as thoughts, feelings, physical sensations and behaviours and see them for what they are, fleeting experiences that come and go naturally. When we do not do this and, instead, get caught up in struggling with them, trying to eradicate them, and judging ourselves for having them, we simply exacerbate our distress. Take Clare, for example, the more she over-identified and struggled with her experiences of stress the more she escalated them.

Clare

There is no denying the fact that Clare had a busy life. She was the mother of three children, two daughters and one son, aged seven, five and two years old respectively. She worked part-time in human resources in a large corporate bank and did some charity work on the weekends with bereaved children. She was a housewife the rest of the time and helped care for her elderly mother who had been suffering with worsening Alzheimer's over the last year. Her eldest children were at school and doing quite well and her son spent most of the time with her throughout the day. It is not surprising that Clare had a few to-do lists on the go at the same time, which she hardly ever felt that she was able to get on top of.

One Thursday morning, after she dropped her daughters off at school, Clare returned home to have a much-needed cup of coffee while she checked her work emails before she intended to begin some of the housework. Her son was a little under the weather with a cough and she wanted to take him to the GP to make sure that everything was OK. As she opened her email account, an email popped up marked as urgent. With some trepidation, Clare opened the email, which was from her manager at work asking her to help out that weekend with finalising a presentation that had to be delivered to a client the following week. Her heart sank; there was no way that she could fit that in on top of all the other tasks she had to get through between now and Sunday.

Clare's thoughts began to race through her mind and she started to get caught up in the content of her thoughts: how am I supposed to do this on top of everything else? I simply cannot do it, but I cannot let them down, they are relying on me and will probably think I cannot handle the job if I say no to this! Maybe I can do it but, then again, I just cannot! As she thought this way and got more caught up in her stressful thoughts, trying to work her problem out, she became more and more emotionally anxious, she then noticed her heart racing in her body and her hands trembling. She felt dizzy, she thought she might be having a heart attack or that her body was failing her generally, so she decided to go and lie down on her bed for a second. As she lay there, she realised that she had left her son playing alone in the TV room. She began to think about what a bad mother she was for taking this action and how, if she lay around all day like this, she was never going to get him to the GP like she had planned. Clare began to feel even more anxious.

As we can see from Clare's example, she experienced stress in four different ways: in her thoughts (I cannot do this), her emotions (anxiety), her bodily sensations (racing heart and trembling hands) and her behaviour (lying on the bed). Instead of allowing these experiences to come and go as they naturally would, she got too caught up with them, tried to get rid of them and judged herself for having them. All this just seemed to lead to higher levels of stress and anxiety.

This habitual reaction to our experiences of stress is common to all of us. If we remain unaware of this automatic response, it is likely to increase our overall stress levels until, eventually, we become completely burnt-out or more depressed and/or anxious. We need to stand back and give space to these experiences (in the form of our thoughts, emotions, sensations and behaviours), take a perspective on them and notice them for what they really are – *they are not us*, but simply passing experiences that we can observe. Mindfulness is exactly how we do just that.

Practice 4.8: I haven't got time for this!

SLOW down

You can use this acronym in any stressful moment, and it will be particularly useful when your busy superhero is clearly in overdrive:

S Stop whatever you are doing and bring your awareness to your breathing.

L Let thoughts, opinions, judgements and urges be.

O Open up your heart, body and mind to what you are feeling.

W Where is most important for you to put your attention right now? (For example taking care of yourself, being present with friends/family, resting the mind, finishing off important work.)

Mindfulness top tips to-go

In this chapter, you have learned how it is helpful to:

▶ Watch your tendency to try to secure everlasting happiness and a blissfully stress-free time (it will only make you busier and more stressed).

▶ Notice how many of your attempts at being less busy can dampen down your rich life experience.

▶ Let go of worrying that there is no time for you, as this will only create the illusion of there being less time.

▶ Switch up old habits to find even more time in the day.

▶ Watch your habitual tendency to over-identify, struggle and get caught up in judgement, with your experiences of stress (in the form of thoughts, feeling, sensations and behaviours).

▶ Try not to buy into unhelpful thoughts (we are going to look more closely at how you can do this in Chapter 6) as they will affect your mood, self-confidence and general stress experience negatively.

▶ SLOW down to manage stress and help you reconnect with what is really important.

5

To be or not to be busy?

Most of us busy people spend a lot of time frantically rushing around on autopilot, unaware of the varied habits that we have that are the real cause of our stress and busyness. As we have seen, these habits come in many forms – we have our:

▶ **busy story** that our minds produce and we tell and repeat to ourselves tirelessly and to anyone else that can bear to listen (I have too much to do, there is no way that I can get all this done in time, it is not fair, my life is overwhelming)!

And we have our:

▶ **superhero fantasies** that we buy into and live by.

These include our:

▶ **perfectionist pursuits, busy behaviours** that are motivated by fear and we use (not so wisely) in an attempt to eradicate all discomfort and bring about everlasting peace and quiet!

We can remain unaware of all that we do that creates our sense of busyness in life. If we want to feel less busy and stressed, then we need to start to wake up to these habitual ways of being. The more we rush around, the more we become increasingly frantic and, as in Sayed's case that follows, this lack of awareness just leads to more agitation and a growing sense of helplessness and hopelessness.

Sayed

Sayed was at his wits' end and run ragged when he came for mindfulness sessions. He explained that he wanted the therapy to take away all his problems. Recently retired, he had planned renovation work on his home and the builders were being unreliable, which he felt really aggrieved about and was taking up much of his time to resolve. Further to this, he was often taking care of his grandchildren, which he felt his son was not appreciative of. His wife was still working, so he found he was often doing many of the household chores.

He spent 40 minutes of his first 50-minute session ranting about how busy he was, how unfair the situation was, how he didn't expect his retirement to be like this, how he was feeling let down, how there just wasn't enough time in the day, how exhausted he was, how his wife didn't understand his stress and how they argued a lot of the time as she thought that he was always complaining– and so on and on! When he wasn't fixated about all this in the session, he was either checking

▶

---

messages on his mobile telephone placed next to him on the couch or answering calls. Here's how some of the therapy conversation went towards the end of this first session:

Psychologist: Well, Sayed, it seems that our time is now up considering that you wanted to end the session earlier than we had scheduled?

Sayed: What? Is that it then? You haven't even said anything, I've been doing all the talking and I don't feel any better for it at all.

Psychologist: Yes, and when you *think* those thoughts, how do you feel right now?

Sayed: Well, even more stressed and like I have wasted my time and still have all this to sort out.

Psychologist: Well this was indeed your time and I can hear that your mind is telling you that you've wasted this precious time and still have so much to do. Although I am sure it seems important for you to focus on those thoughts and to talk about how awful everything is for you right now; and that it seems crucial to you to check and answer your telephone as often as you do, I wonder if you weren't *thinking* those thoughts and doing all that then you might feel slightly differently right now. I wonder if all that stuff was not in the way, then you may have had a different experience coming here today.

We have already seen that, when we feel blocked on our way and our stress level rises, simply noticing the process of ranting in our mind is a great way to come back to the present moment where there is no stress – just this one breath, just this one moment, just this ranting. If you are stuck in a queue somewhere or waiting for a delayed train and getting stressed and angry, simply notice that reaction. You then have a choice to keep the frustration alive or do something else more productive and worthwhile with that time (sounds like a great opportunity to practise some mindfulness to us). Remember, mindfulness helps to improve our decision making; it allows us to use our time effectively, as we base our life choices and actions on the clarity that comes from awareness and considering what might be most helpful to do right now, rather than allowing habitual reactions (such as ranting) to drive our actions.

Next time you wake up to your mind's ranting about being held back and delayed, how about getting mindful of your phone, tablet or whatever device you have at hand. We know you would probably have one of these in some form or another handy – what the hell would we do without our trusty gadgets to take us away from our boredom and frustrations? The common reality is that often we become more frustrated once we have pulled them out from our pocket and been bombarded with the endless messages and emails we feel compelled to respond to – *immediately*! So, how about doing something completely different with your mobile phone?

The purpose of the next exercise is to get acquainted with your mobile phone, like you may never have before, a bit like a young child would curiously admire a present that she has just received for her birthday. It is all about reinforcing the ability that you have within yourself to break habits and act in accordance with how you wish to behave (mindfully), rather than be dictated to by some other fearful or uncomfortable part of yourself (that usually may motivate you to constantly check your messages as soon as your phone is in sight or you are bored and frustrated being delayed somewhere).

The intention of the exercise is to cultivate a non-judging awareness of your experience of your phone, nothing more and nothing less; to pay attention to your mobile phone and to your experience of your touch and sight of it.

Practice 5.1: I haven't got time for this!

Getting acquainted with your mobile phone

▷ First sit, with your mobile phone on a table or other surface in front of you or become aware of it in your pocket.

▷ Reach out and lift your phone up in your hand, notice its weight and acknowledge how your hand and body is now one phone heavier.

▷ Next, while you hold your phone in your hand, gently move it around, flipping it over in the palm of your hand, using your fingers, thumb and hand, notice how its weight becomes lighter and heavier on different parts of your fingers and hands.

▷ There is the weight of the phone and then there is you, noticing its weight.

▷ Allow its weight to take centre stage in your awareness.

▷ Now, hold your phone still once again, allow it to rest in the palm of your hand and now run your thumb over its surface in all directions, notice the texture, the smoothness versus the bumps and indentations.

▶ It is natural for your attention to wander or become distracted, when this happens just gently guide it back to noticing the sensations of your phone in your hand.

▶ Be aware that you are noticing your phone in this moment.

▶ There is your phone and then there is you, noticing it and your experiences of it.

▶ Now gaze upon your phone, exploring it with your eyes and sight, noticing its contours, edges, colours and markings.

▶ Notice the space around your phone and where this space meets its edges.

▶ Notice its sleek design with wonder and curiosity.

▶ As you move your phone around in your hand again, notice where the light is reflected, where it shimmers and fades across its surface.

▶ Should your attention wander or become distracted, perhaps by thoughts about your phone, what emails, messages you may have received on it, simply acknowledge the distraction and then gently guide your attention back to noticing your experiences of your phone.

▶ Your experiences of your phone change – but the part of you that notices these experiences does not change, it remains constant – simply aware.

How do you do 'busy'?

Sayed found it useful to ask himself the following questions, some of which you may also find helpful to think about and answer for yourself. We have added some tips for you to have a go at answering them. Try this exercise now, and have a think about your answers.

Practice 5.2: Mindfulness right now!

How to be a busy bee like me

▶ What is my busy story (it is not fair, I have so much to do, others are getting in the way, etc.)?

▶ Does this story have any themes (focusing on past, future, failure, rejection, injustice, judging, criticising self or others)?

▶ Do I think about how busy I am in any specific context or all contexts of my life (work, home, relationships)?

▶ What do I do when I am stressed and busy (shout, rush about, check my phone/emails, fidget, etc.)?

▶ What do others notice about me when I am busy (I am argumentative, snappy, disinterested, disconnected, accusatory, distracted, talking fast, talking over others)?

▶ How do others respond to me when I am *doing* busy (comfort me, spend time with me – we guess not)?

▶ How do I respond to others when they point out my stress and busyness (tell them to shut up, they do not understand, withdraw from them)?

The busy story-telling mind

The busy stories produced by our minds might come in the form of words in a sentence structure or images, pictures and scenarios being played out in our thinking minds. When stressed, you may be thinking about the past, regretfully, about all the things that should have happened, memories about all that went wrong. Or you may be thinking to the future, in catastrophic terms, about all the terrible things that might happen! Or you may have fantasies in your mind about how things should be; judgements, criticisms and expectations about yourself or the world around you.

It is all too easy to get hooked by the compelling thoughts produced by our minds and that can have a significant impact on how we feel and behave. If, however, you were to unhook yourself from all these thoughts, by simply noticing the process of thinking (more on this in the next chapter), you may find that the moment you are in is quite bearable, even quite pleasant or that something new may arise that you might not have even noticed or had the clarity of mind to act upon whilst being caught up in all this noise in your mind. Mindfulness gives us this opportunity – to unhook ourselves and stand back from our stressful thoughts, our busy story-producing minds and to truly fully appreciate this moment, just how it really is!

My life is too busy to not think!

Really? This is a common fear we hear from our busy clients, that their life is bound to fall apart if they stop thinking (there is another worrying thought to notice right there, we would say). Well, we are not here to advocate that you try to stop thinking altogether; in fact, you would get very frustrated and even more stressed if you tried or expected yourself to be able to. Thinking is, of course, helpful, and problem-solving and analysing are useful if they remain focused and productive. In fact, the greatest achievements of mankind, such as space travel, industry, telecommunications and the internet are all testaments to our intelligence and proficiency at problem-solving – but there is a large difference between thinking through a problem constructively and the futility and stress that endless worry and rumination brings.

Consider the following story and how, sometimes, no matter how many questions we ask, we may never find the answer we are looking for and, usually, we would find it more helpful just to let go, accept that we may not know, that there is nothing to solve or work out here, and get on with something more worthwhile. Ahh, freedom ...

A young child once asked his teacher, 'Teacher, what is it that holds the earth up in space?' The teacher replied, 'Oh, that would be the really large bear that holds the earth on the tip of his nose.' 'Ah, I see', replied the inquisitive child, 'but what then holds up the large bear, that holds the earth up on the tip of its nose, up in space?' 'That would be the even larger fish that holds up the bear on the tip of its fin.' 'Oh, I see teacher,' the child replied again, 'but then what holds the larger fish up, that holds the bear that holds the earth up in space?' 'Child, it's bears and fish all the way down ...'

It is only through awareness, and noticing the process of thinking in your mind, that you can make decisions about how useful your thinking might be to you in any given moment. Irrespective of whether a thought is true or not, the real question to be asking yourself is: is thinking this thought, right now, helpful to me? Is it helping me to live the kind of life that I want? Is it helping me do what is most important to me right now? Is it helping me be the person I really want to be in this situation?

Practice 5.3: Mindfulness right now!

Think tank

Bring to mind a thought or worry that, perhaps, you have been mulling over in your mind recently. As you bring your awareness to these thoughts, begin to ask yourself, how does ruminating, worrying, analysing and focusing on these thoughts:

- ▶ Make me feel emotionally?
- ▶ Make me feel physically?
- ▶ Affect my behaviour?
- ▶ Affect my relationships?
- ▶ Interfere with my precious time?
- ▶ Make me more efficient?
- ▶ Help me to enjoy this moment?
- ▶ Help me to create a satisfying life?
- ▶ Help me to get ahead, reach my goals and what is really important to me, in this situation, right now?

Stop with the positives!

Once we identify that a thought or a particular pattern of thinking is not working too well for us, usually we would try to stop it, by attempting to push it out of our mind either by distracting ourselves from it and/or trying to think the opposite or a more positive alternative thought to counter it.

However, trying to push stressful thoughts out of our mind by thinking the opposite or positively about a situation is often a circular, effortful, time-consuming and tiring experience. Perhaps you have tried that yourself (most of us tend to do it) and also recognise how often it does not get you anywhere in the long run, except more stressed out. The more we try to push thoughts out of our mind, the more they tend to pop back in. It is a well-known phenomenon in psychology called the rebound effect. Much like throwing a tennis ball against a wall, the harder we throw it, the faster it bounces back!

Sure, thinking positively does work sometimes and, often, in the short term, bringing us some relief but it is only a matter of time before our minds produce another counterargument in response to that positive thought. It is a bit like playing a game of chess ...

Checkmate!

Imagine that your negative thoughts are the black pieces on a chessboard while your positive thoughts are the white pieces. As a black piece moves forwards, perhaps saying something like, 'I'm too busy,' 'I'll never get this done in time,' 'I have so much to do, life is so unfair,' often we react by instinctively pushing a white piece onto the board to counter this, perhaps saying something like, 'It's OK, I do not have to get it all done straight away,' 'Other people are just as busy as me,' etc.

The problem with this approach is that every white piece attracts another black piece and vice versa, and this is no ordinary game of chess as there are an infinite number of black pieces as there are white ones. The consequence is that this battle can go on and on forever, it is endless, leaving us tired, exhausted, stressed out and feeling like we are going around in circles. It is also extremely time-consuming and often takes us away from doing something that we may prefer to be doing or spending our time in a more meaningful and productive way. What is more, there is only ever one loser in this game of chess as all the pieces are yours! Attempting to dominate the board with white pieces is a common experience for us all and perhaps this resonates for you?

So, how can we break this habit and step away from the battle? Well, first consider that if the black and white pieces are your thoughts, what part of this game of chess is actually *you*? What if you were the chessboard itself, which is firm, strong, stable and secure and reaches out in all directions and simply holds all these pieces? The board is not involved in this tiring battle and has ample space for all the pieces, it remains unaffected by the pieces and the strenuous battle they are having. Mindfulness is the tool to help you to be more like this chessboard when you notice your mind's endless and often futile attempts to push out stressful thoughts while getting caught up in this game of black versus white. Being more like the board means that these stressful thoughts simply pass through you.

Practice 5.4: Mindfulness right now!

Tying yourself in (k)nots

This simple exercise is intended to amuse and, more importantly, to show you how all your hard work spent trying to get rid of thoughts and feelings by trying to think positively or by trying to distract yourself from them is never going to pay off. Try really, really hard at the following tasks:

▶ Do not think of a pink elephant with black and yellow spots.

▶ Think of the dog/cat/goldfish/mother-in-law dying – feel nothing.

▶ Think of winning the lottery – feel nothing, do not imagine what you could do with the cash.

▶ Look in the mirror and have no negative thoughts at all, ever again.

▶ Do not think about how stressful this exercise is, when you have so many more important things to do.

Patterns in the mind

Neuroscience helps us to understand that our brains create networks of thoughts (neurological connections and pathways). One thought is associated with another; so, one thought may ignite further thoughts (there is no black without white, see what we mean?). An arm of behavioural science (called relational frame theory) also helps us to understand how as humans we learn to use language and thought and, specifically, how we derive relations between objects, events and symbolic representations held in our minds. In essence, all this helps to explain how our minds develop intricate stories or scripts, if you like, which, as we know, can cause us undue stress and, as importantly, prove to be life-limiting and quite unhelpful when it comes to our experience of busyness. Much like a computer, we hold these stories, or networks/programmes in mind but, very much unlike a computer, we cannot delete these programmes, ever.

So, what can we do if certain thoughts and stories are stressing us out? Well, the good news is that our brains are 'plastic'. What?! Yes. An amazing discovery from neuroscience called *neuroplasticity* helps us to understand that our brains are not fixed or static and we can create new neural pathways, if we chose to. The fundamental principle here is that our brain changes and adapts in response to what we experience and how we choose to train it and those changes impact how we think, feel and behave. Every time we experience or do something new, we create a new neural pathway or synapse and, then, the more we exercise that specific neural pathway, the more we reinforce it, making it more likely that we will travel down that pathway again. In essence, we can rewire our brains via mindfulness practice. We can stop strengthening the programme or thinking networks that are causing us stress, we can wake up to when we are thinking them, see them for what they are – just thoughts, just the process of thinking, just a busy story (rather than listening to the content of them and then acting on the back of them).

Once we do this, and continue to do this, via our mindfulness practice, we strengthen a new neural pathway – training our minds to be present, right here and right now, rather than caught up in the compelling thoughts and stories produced by our minds, freeing us up to move towards aspects of our lives that matter most to us. We will also become aware of, and develop insight into, our own mental habits and patterns and be able to quickly recognise these, to unhook and step back from them. Simple, but not so easy, it is a discipline that needs to be practised and, the more we practise, the more natural it will become and the more we benefit.

Here is another quick mindfulness exercise that you can use when you find yourself caught up in your busy story. It will help to reduce all the futile worry connected with this story, really helping you to get out of your head and back in to the world around you.

Practice 5.5: I haven't got time for this!

Sound advice

▶ Wherever you are, stop what you are doing in your mind and turn your attention towards your breathing to anchor you in this present moment. If it helps to sharpen your sense of hearing, close your eyes.

▶ Be still and notice what you can hear. Not so much searching for sounds but receiving sounds from near and far, as if your ears were a microphone, simply picking up sounds.

▶ Listen with curiosity, opening your awareness up to quiet, loud, soft and harsh sounds. Notice what is here, right now. Perhaps, sounds of traffic, sounds of electronic devices, sounds of people talking, sounds of leaves rustling, sounds of breathing.

▶ If any judgments or opinions come to mind about these sounds, allow these, too, to enter your awareness and gently let them pass by as you return your attention to the sensory quality of sounds.

▶ Rest your full attention on one sound. Notice which direction the sound is coming from, whether it is moving or still. Notice how far away the sound is, close by or perhaps in the distance. Notice how loud it appears, whether it changes in volume with each moment, or whether it stays constant. Notice the tone and pitch of the sound and how it changes with each passing moment.

▶ Allow the sound to fade from your awareness and reconnect with your breathing.

▶ If your eyes were closed, slowly open them, thanking your mind for this experience.

Mindfulness top tips to-go

In this chapter, you have learned that it is helpful to:

▶ Pay attention to your busy automatic tendencies, such as your busy story and busy behaviours.

▶ Engage less with this story and all the busy behaviours that you do, as your life will just feel busier and you will start to feel helpless to change it.

▶ Recognise that positive thinking and distracting yourself in the face of stressful thoughts often just makes us more stressed and is life-limiting and time-consuming.

▶ Stand back, be more mindful and bring more awareness to your thoughts.

▶ Let go of your busy tendencies while bringing your awareness to your present moment experience, which will free up space and energy for you to get ahead and focus your attention on more meaningful experiences in life.

Busy doing nothing
(at all helpful, anyway!)

You may already, with the help of the previous chapters, have identified your particular fantasies, habitual stories and busy-bee behaviours and how these connect to your levels of stress and illusions of escape from this. As we now start to notice these habits using mindfulness, our awareness gradually increases, we begin to pay attention to the power of our thoughts … so what do we do now? Surely we need to *do* something? Escape these unbearable thoughts, feelings or sensations? Instead of adding more to our to-do list, let us try something really different!

Practice 6.1: Mindfulness right now!

Watching your thoughts

We ask that you just take a few moments before you read on:

- ▶ To rest in awareness as you have started to learn to do already.
- ▶ See if you can notice what thoughts are going through your mind as you read this right now.
- ▶ You might hear thoughts and your mind saying things like: *What's the point in this? How is this going to help? I've got to finish reading this quickly! I can't concentrate, this is too difficult. I've got other more pressing things to be getting on with* … or any other thoughts at all.
- ▶ Go on, despite what your mind may be telling you, despite what thoughts may be getting in the way, try it right now for a couple of minutes, see if you can drop in to watch and notice any similar (or any different) thoughts at all going through your mind, before you read on.

So, how did you do? Did you notice any of the thoughts that showed up in your mind? If so, congratulate yourself – you were just being *mindful!* What thoughts did you notice, were they similar to the ones above? Perhaps they were unrelated to the exercise or the book and about something completely different. Perhaps you noticed very few or no thoughts at all. Whatever you noticed is fine, congratulate yourself for noticing the process of your thinking mind, as that was the task after all.

Now, if you did notice thoughts in your mind, consider what impact these thoughts were having on your experience in the moment before you became aware of them: how did they make you feel? Did they affect the way you felt emotionally and/or physically? How did they help or hinder your progress in reading this book or anything else you might be doing?

Did they encourage you to put the book down or keep reading? What was it like not to do anything with them, just to watch them go by? Our thoughts can be very powerful, especially when we get hooked by what they are saying, without much awareness of being caught up in them. Unhelpfully, they can affect our mood, our bodies and how we behave. When we are under the control of our thoughts and they are in the driving seat, so to speak, they can influence our behaviour dramatically, taking us further away from living the life that we may want for ourselves.

Unhooking from worry and stressful thoughts

As we covered earlier, stressful thoughts will come and go, passing through our awareness on their own accord, naturally. But what tends to happen more often when we are not being aware is that we get caught up in our thoughts, which can have a detrimental impact on our stress levels and our actions. We can start to behave in ways that move us further away from the kind of person we would prefer to be or the kind of life we would prefer to be living.

This is what was happening to Mark, as you will discover below.

Mark

Mark, a vice-president in a large corporate bank, came for mindfulness sessions after he noticed that he was becoming increasingly anxious at work. The bank was going through a major restructuring and lots of people were being made redundant. He had noticed how his performance at work had declined, he was unable to concentrate and was becoming increasingly more stressed and short-tempered with his team. He knew that he could not go on like this and feared that, if his situation did not improve, he was bound to receive a bad review and might even lose his job. He had recovered from a bout of depression some two years ago and had also suffered a redundancy in a previous job; he did not want to live through either experience again. Here is how some of the conversation went:

Psychologist: What thoughts show up in your mind when you are trying to get work done in the office?

➤

Mark: Well, I never thought about my thoughts before, I suppose that I'm thinking, I can't concentrate and I can't do this! I'll never get everything done – I have so much to do! What's wrong with me? I shouldn't have made those mistakes! I am going to lose my job again!

Psychologist: And what emotions show up while you get caught up in thoughts like, 'I am going to lose my job'? Do you feel them now?

Mark: Well, I start to feel really anxious and angry. Yes, just thinking about this now is making me feel anxious.

Psychologist: I see, and where do you notice those feelings the most in your body?

Mark: Well, all over my body, I suppose. I feel really tense right now, in my chest area. Sometimes, I start trembling, feel nauseous. It's difficult to catch my breath at times. I even snapped a pen in my hand the other day out of frustration!

Psychologist: I see, and what about other thoughts, what other thoughts do you notice that your mind can give you when you are in that situation?

Mark: Well, I start thinking that others are laughing at me, it's humiliating to be in this state. I think that I won't be able to find another job and I won't be able to enjoy what I really love to do. I think that I will have to sell my home and I have let my family down.

Psychologist: I understand, and what about your behaviour? How does your behaviour change, and what do you feel like doing when you keep thinking, 'I am going to lose my job' and experience those unpleasant feelings?

Mark: Well, as I said, I get tense and can shout at my team. I sometimes rush off to the toilet to try to compose myself. I can't concentrate at all and I get no work done, really! I become ineffective and useless.

Psychologist: Well, despite the thought 'I am going to lose my job' being understandable and, possibly, true, it sounds like it isn't at all helpful to keep thinking about it and getting caught up in it when it pops up in your mind, especially when you're at work, if it is really important to you to keep your job, that is.

Sometimes, our thoughts are very convincing and compelling, they are very good at hooking us in. Sometimes, there is some truth to back them up. We do not suggest you spend your time trying to convince yourselves otherwise, trying to challenge or provide a counter-argument to what your mind is giving you (as we saw in the previous chapter). Instead, as we have said, when stressful thoughts do show up, we encourage you to ask yourself the following:

▶ Is it really *helpful* to keep thinking it, at this time and in this situation?

▶ Does thinking it help you to move towards the life that you want, that you really care about?

The more we allow ourselves to get caught up in thoughts in an autopilot fashion – worrying about 'catastrophic' eventualities such as losing our jobs, failing to get everything done or anything else – the more our stress levels increase and the more changes in our behaviour and functioning occur and these changes may, in fact, take us further away from what matters most to us in any given situation.

In Mark's case, getting caught up in his thoughts without any awareness that this is what he was doing, made it more likely he became ineffective at work, that others would notice a drop in his performance and that job loss would, inevitably, follow. It might seem counter-intuitive not to but, for Mark, buying into his worry about losing his job eventually may have become self-fulfilling.

Being pushed around by thoughts!

As mentioned earlier, an arm of behavioural science (called relational frame theory) provides us with an account of how, as humans, we learn to use thought and language. It helps us to understand that the human mind has the amazing ability to form symbolic representations of everything it encounters and can also then make use of these representations later on. This allows us to think about things and experience them beyond what we can see, hear, smell, taste and touch within any given moment. For example, thinking about ticking off all the items on your to-do list and then lying on a beach in a few weeks' time can make you feel excited. Remembering a scary scene from the horror film you watched last week can leave you feeling scared as you fall asleep (or, as in Mark's case, thinking about losing his job can make him feel anxious and tense as he tries to get work done).

Basically, we can react to an idea in our heads as if it were happening right now, in this very moment. What is more, we also create links between these representations held in our mind. For example, if you learned that a new TV programme was even scarier than the film you saw, you may be afraid to watch it, despite never having actually seen it. For Mark, thinking back to his previous bout of depression and losing his job before, made him even more anxious around the thought of being made redundant this time. The ability to react to ideas and situations in our minds, which we have never actually experienced, provides us with significant benefits, particularly as we are able to problem-solve tricky situations that we may not be encountering right now. However, it also means that, sometimes, we forget that we are dealing with a representation in our mind rather than the real deal. We can become paralysed with fear just thinking about something that might go wrong in the future or crippled with shame by regretting what we may have done in the past. We can become trapped, immobilised and behaviourally ineffective when falling under the control of the thoughts and language produced by our minds. We become psychologically rigid and stuck in our ways. It is as if our thoughts have come to own us rather than us owning our thoughts!

Short-circuiting the thinking mind

The truth is that we might not be able to stop thoughts popping into our mind, but we certainly have a choice about what kind of attention we give to them when they do. If you had the thought, *I am a green alien from outer space*, the chances are that you would laugh that thought off without paying any real attention to it at all (we assume, but if you do have this thought and do not find yourself laughing it off, that is OK, too).

But, like Mark, if you noticed a thought that presented some threat to your downfall in life, suggesting something about your failure or rejection in some area of your life – such as *I am fat, I am ugly, I will never get all this done today, I am going to lose my job* – then you would be more likely to pay lots of attention to it. This attention is driven by our inherent survival mechanism (see Chapter 4 to refresh yourself on this), which is programmed to believe that if we do not pay attention to the threat (content of that thought) and try to work it out somehow then it is bound to get worse and lead to our downfall.

It may surprise you to know that you have the ability within you to treat any thought that may show up in your mind in the same way that you would treat the thought *I am a green alien from outer space*, which is a really helpful skill to have, if certain thoughts are causing you stress and getting in the way of what you want to achieve in life and what you want your life to be about. You simply do not have to pay attention to or think the thoughts in your mind if you choose not to, when it seems helpful not to. Wow! Amazing!

We know, right? *Well how do I do that?* Before we take a look at how we can develop more of the ability to unhook from our stressful thoughts, let us just take a moment to gain a better understanding of how our minds work by taking a closer look at the amazing world that goes on in our heads.

The hamster mind

As we mentioned previously, we have two modes of our mind: the *thinking mind* and the *awareness/observing mind*. We now want to encourage you to consider your thinking mind as a very busy hamster, frantically and endlessly running on its wheel. Because what is also certain about our thinking mind is that it is a creature of habit, reinforcing its same pattern of busy behaviour throughout our lives.

Our hamster (thinking) mind is on autopilot in very much the same way as the many other habits that we tend to find ourselves running through automatically each day, such as our morning ablutions, our journey to and from work, rushing around to get everything done, etc. Much like the varied behaviours that make up these daily tasks, there is also a pattern of intricate and connecting thoughts (patterns of thoughts as we discussed in the previous chapter) that occur in our thinking minds that we remain mostly unaware of as they continue to tick away on autopilot each day. Our thinking mind is a problem-solver – much like a hamster, busy doing, analysing, trying to reach the end of its wheel, trying to find an end result and work everything out.

Now, as we have said, this problem-solving habit of the thinking mind is all very good when we have a practical problem to solve, such as how do we get

from A to B. In fact, without the problem-solving habit of the thinking mind, we might never have learned how to get ourselves dressed as a child, been able to find our way to and from work as an adult or sniff out the tastiest seeds as a hamster. This problem-solving approach to our lives is forever reinforced amidst our busy days and often within the technical aspects of our work. It helps us to navigate ourselves through the entirety of tasks to get things ticked off on our to-do lists (yes, those again!), often with much success.

It is quite understandable, therefore, when we have an emotional problem (like Mark in the earlier example), that instinctively we would apply the same tried-and-tested problem-solving approach to navigate our way out of it in an attempt to get rid of it – we feel the need to evaluate it, to understand where this problem has come from, where it is going, what we need to prepare ourselves for in the face of it. This is completely understandable and natural (but usually unhelpful).

As we saw, Mark's instinctive tendency to think through his emotional problem in this way just seemed to escalate and worsen it even more – his thinking mind was not helping him to resolve his situation (emotional 'problem') at all – he just became more anxious and irritable as a result. He noticed that his mood had worsened and his functioning and behaviour declined. In true testament to this thinking mind, he began to ruminate and worry on past negative experiences, what had been going wrong, all that he could not do, and what negative eventualities might materialise and where this all might end up for him once again. As he thought through his problem in this way, his mood and performance deteriorated. Imagine your hamster, running faster on the wheel, perhaps believing that the cat is coming: but running faster to escape is not the answer!

Our problem-solving mind is not going to solve an emotional 'problem', no matter how hard it tries – after all, emotions are not a problem to be solved, they are a condition of life and, therefore, they do not have a solution. The habitual behaviour of our hamster minds is, in fact, the real problem that we have to deal with.

Watching thoughts come and go

Touching a thought that pops up into our thinking mind with awareness is like touching a soap bubble; the impact that the thought has on our behaviour often *vanishes*. The simple and beautiful reality is that we cannot be both in our thinking mode of mind (running on our hamster wheel) and our awareness mode of mind (noticing the hamster frantically running) at the same time, in the same moment – it is humanly impossible. In other words, as soon as we 'wake up' and notice that our hamster is frantically running around its wheel, simultaneously we slow down the hamster on its tracks. With each moment of awareness that we bring to our thoughts, we reinforce the behaviour of noticing, slowing down the hamster, moment by moment.

Human being rather than human doing

Mark thought that this all sounded great, but asked what he should do with the thought once he had noticed it. As we have outlined, *nothing*, that is it – noticing is all we have to do. We are so programmed in a way to do something that it is understandable that, like Mark, we feel a bit weird about doing nothing and believe that surely there is something else that needs to be done. Remember, you are cultivating a totally new way of being and relating to your experience and, specifically, your thoughts in this instance, it will feel unusual at first.

Simply noticing and becoming aware of our thoughts, rather than trying to challenge them with positive thoughts or push them out altogether is the way that we can gain some relief from the stress and busyness produced by our minds. As we become aware of our thoughts, we simply 'sit' and be with them as they are, letting go of our natural tendency to resolve these thoughts, come up with an answer or find a solution.

Being with our thoughts in this way helps to lessen the emotional impact of them in that moment – we are not exacerbating them or making them worse by struggling with them – instead, we are noticing and accepting them for what they are (thoughts, stories, sounds, images, experiences in our mind). Furthermore, we are freeing up the natural tendency for our thoughts to come and then to pass by of their own accord, as they will naturally. We now have abundant space with which to experience and actually live our lives, in this very moment, allowing us to get on with, savour and gain greater pleasure from what is worthwhile and fulfilling to us. This is the difference between a *human doing* mode and a *human being* mode.

Try the following practice to notice the difference between these two modes right now. In the first part of this next practice, you will be *doing*; thinking, judging, analysing, perhaps even worrying whilst, in the second part, you will practise simply *being* with sensations and thoughts that arise.

Practice 6.2: Mindfulness right now!

Being human

Part 1 Human doing

▶ Spend a few moments thinking about your hands.

▶ Perhaps judging your hands, whether you like or dislike them. Perhaps thinking what about them you would like to change. Perhaps thinking about how your hands help you in your day-to-day life or whether they have caused you any problems.

▶ Continue thinking about your hands, allowing thoughts to arise naturally.

Try out these steps before continuing on to the next part.

Part 2 Human being

▶ Close your eyes to help bring your attention in towards your body.

▶ Bring your awareness down your arms and in to your hands. Tune in to the sensations that are in your hands right now. Allow your awareness to encompass the entirety of your hands, from the surface of the skin, down in to the tissue and the bones. Notice the palm of the hands, the back of the hands and down the fingers in to the finger tips.

▶ Notice the sensation of touch, whatever your hands are resting against. Perhaps noticing a sense of warmth or moisture at the surface of the skin, a sense of tingling at the finger tips. Noticing whatever arises, as it is.

▶ If any thoughts arise, thoughts about your hands, this practice, thoughts about the book, thoughts about your busy to-do list, notice these thoughts as they are without becoming caught up in them, challenging them or pushing them away and redirect your attention back to the sensations in your hands.

▶ Clench your fists and explore what happens to the entirety of your hands. Relax the muscle and notice the sensations changing with each moment.

Back away from the brick wall

With mindfulness, we are able to stand back, distance and disconnect ourselves from the content of our thoughts and see them exactly for what they are – streams of words, sentences, images, pictures or events in our mind, passing by in our awareness.

As we have seen, what we do, instinctively and usually, is get caught up in them and what they may somehow be telling us and assume that they represent some real danger or threat. We might find ourselves scurrying through these thoughts and images like Mystic Meg looking into her tea leaves, attempting to glean portends about the future; no matter how compelling this seems, it is about as effective as trying to dig yourself out of a hole. Save yourself the trouble of consulting an old quack (your thoughts) and let them drift off in their own time into the ether.

You do not need to waste so much energy figuring 'it all' out – this is really stressful for you and it does not work well anyway. And, as hard and tricky as it seems to resist meddling in your thoughts and instead to distance yourself from them, the pay-off is that, after all these years of banging your head against a brick wall, finally you notice how painful it has been and that you have a headache – plus you are still no closer to 'the answer'. Now, you know, and we have already told you there is no answer, so back away from the wall and see how much of a relief it is to let go of it all.

Practice 6.3: I haven't got time for this!

Never mind your mind

▶ To help you distance yourself from thoughts, you can try to imagine that they are the voices of some noisy school children playing up in the back of the car, teasing and judging you, as you drive them to school. They may be shouting: 'You're going the wrong way – you'll never get us to school on time!' Your natural tendency may be to slam your foot onto the brake and turn around to the children and tell them to be quiet and argue back: 'I know exactly where I am going and we will be there in good time.' Of course, the more you do that, the more fuel you are adding to the fire, encouraging them to argue back with you some more. Instead, what you *can* do is keep your foot on the accelerator and your eyes on the road ahead of you, ignoring the teasing that you can hear, although remaining aware of it in the back of the car and, eventually, soon enough, the children (your unhelpful thoughts) will quieten down, leaving you free to pursue and efficiently complete your task of getting them to school on time (or whatever your goal in reality may be).

▶ You may also try to imagine that your thoughts are like the sound coming from the radio as you are busy getting on with the housework or some other task at work. So, if someone asked you what the radio show was all about, you may reply that, although you heard that the radio was on in the background, you did not pay much attention to it at all.

▶ You could imagine that you are standing at the side of a busy city road and that your thoughts are all the taxis whizzing past you – just remember as you stand there watching them in this way not to jump into the back of one to catch a ride.

▶ A busy mind could also be considered like a handful of coloured helium balloons or a flock of birds chattering in a tree, ready to rise one by one or all together into the skies.

▶ You could also imagine that there are leaves floating down a flowing stream in front of you and that each time a stressful thought shows up in your mind that you place that thought on one of the leaves and watch it float away.

▶ You may also like to label your thoughts as they show up in your mind throughout the day – you may silently say to yourself: *thinking* to allow yourself to stand back from them and notice them for what they really are – just events, sounds, images passing through your awareness.

With all these ways of seeing and responding to your thoughts, it is important to recognise that your thoughts may come and go, they may change, become louder or quieter, show up more frequently or infrequently but, while all this is happening in your thinking mind, your awareness remains unaffected by these changes. Your awareness has enough room to hold all these changing thoughts, and you can expand your awareness to focus also on whatever task you want to get on with instead.

If, on the other hand, you allow your attention to get caught up in thoughts, maybe analysing or struggling with the content of what they are saying, do not be surprised if you end up in a place that you do not want to be in at all – you will be on the first fast train out of here, straight to stressville, but that is OK also, because there are no one-way tickets to anywhere when it comes to mindfulness – the present moment is always there for us to return to at any time!

Practice 6.4: Mindfulness right now!

I am bigger than my thoughts

As you did at the start of this chapter, have another go at reinforcing your ability to watch your thoughts with this practice right now and as you are on the go. Just follow the simple steps outlined below:

▶ Freeze right now.
▶ Watch your thoughts arise in your mind for one minute (do not count the time, just take a rough guess at how long a minute is while you do this).
▶ Notice your thoughts.
▶ No need to stop your thoughts.
▶ Let your thoughts come, see them go; use one of the metaphors or labelling techniques from above to help you do this.

When doing this exercise, you may have noticed some similar thoughts to *I'm too busy to do this, What a load of tosh, I feel stupid, This is a really long minute, What would my boss say if s/he knew I was doing this?, I feel so chilled – this is it!, Been doing this for ten seconds and it still isn't working, What shall I have for tea?* or anything else at all. Whether you noticed the presence or absence of any thoughts, congratulate yourself, you were being mindful.

If you find this hard or do not notice any thoughts, do not be concerned, discouraged or give up, just give the exercise another go when you have a few minutes to spare. Remember, this is a drastically different way of being from usual that will come with patience and practice. You may also find the technique in the next practice helpful.

Practice 6.5: Mindfulness right now!

Stepping off the hamster wheel back into reality

▶ Think of a thought that stresses you out. It might be: *I am never going to get all this stuff done in time,* or the like.

▶ Spend a moment or two thinking your stressful thought, silently repeating it to yourself in your mind, really buying into it.

▶ Notice how stressed you can feel as a result of letting this thought get its teeth into you.

▶ Now, repeat the thought but, this time, add a few 'mindful' words before it. These mindful words are, '*I notice that I am having the thought that …*', so it might sound like: *I notice that I am having the thought that I am never going to get this stuff done in time* (or whatever your stressful thought was). Repeat the thought with these few words added before it, a few times silently.

▶ Notice what happens – did you feel any sense of distance between you and your stressful thought? Did your level of stress change at all? (Remember, if it did, this is just a fortunate by-product of using this present moment awareness technique.)

When using these techniques, it may be only one second (or less!) before your thinking mind pipes up once again to replay the stressful thought (or another one) and captures your attention with it once again, and that is OK. All you have to do is repeat one of the techniques above. It is important to remember that these techniques are not designed to stop the stressful thoughts occurring, to make them occur less frequently or to make you feel less stressed (these are just fortunate by-products, should they occur).

These techniques really help to wake us up, in any given moment, to the fact that we might be running on autopilot, getting hooked by the products of our thinking minds, replaying stressful thoughts over and over again, worsening our stress level and, perhaps, behaving in ways that move us further away from the life we would prefer to have or the person we would prefer to be. The result is that immediately we stand back and gain perspective on our thinking mind as we step into our awareness mind. This provides us with greater choice about how to behave (rather than allowing our thoughts to determine the direction we go in) and frees up the time, energy and space to move forwards with what is most important to us in that very moment.

Mindfulness top tips to-go

In this chapter, you have learned that it is helpful to:

▶ See how powerful thoughts can be and how getting caught up in them can have an unhelpful impact on our stress levels and move us away from what matters to us most.

▶ Not get caught up in unhelpful thoughts; it is futile, time-consuming, makes us inefficient and often leads us away from reaching our goals and the life we want.

▶ Understand the habitual behaviour of your hamster mind.

▶ Use specific techniques to notice and unhook from your thoughts (rather than always reinforcing the stressful patterns in your thinking mind) and to reduce stress.

▶ Connect to your present life experience to get out of your head and back to enjoying your reality.

Our thoughts are the winds and our emotion the waters ... The average length of an emotion left to its own devices is 1.5 minutes. What keeps it going beyond that? ... the winds of thought.

Tara Brach, psychologist

Tracking your practice

In Part 2 we have covered a number of mindfulness practices. We invite you to pick out as many of the following practices as you like. Like any skill, the more you practise the more you will cultivate and embody mindfulness in your day-to-day life, even when you are not purposefully practising. Having said that, thinking about doing all of these practices might seem overwhelming and it could be that you just want to turn the page and keep reading. We understand that, so it is really important to be aware that even a small amount of mindfulness practice can have a significant affect over time. It is also very normal for people starting out in practising mindfulness to dip in and out of the practices, and that is fine also. Please choose whatever feels comfortable for you and, remember, you can always come back to these practices to try them out again.

As before, feel free to make any notes of what you tried out, what you found more or less easy or what made it difficult to do. In addition, if you find yourself beating yourself up for not doing enough practice or not doing it right somehow, notice those thoughts and bring yourself gently back to your breath.

Practice	Page	When?	Notes
4.3: Wake up and smell the coffee	41	Any time you take a break.	
4.5: Spending time with yourself wherever you are	45	At regular intervals throughout the day. Perhaps set a reminder on your phone.	
4.6: Watching time – tick tock!	46	When you go to check the time.	

Practice	Page	When?	Notes
4.7: Changing old habits	48	Once a week; consider one thing you could do differently this week.	
4.8: SLOW down	52	When you are feeling particularly stressed and busy, use this acronym as a helpful reminder.	
5.1: Getting acquainted with your mobile phone	58	Any time you habitually reach for your phone, perhaps when you are bored, waiting or feeling held back.	
5.3: Think tank	62	Any moment you are feeling particularly busy.	
5.5: Sound advice	65	Perhaps try this when you are caught up in any of your busy stories.	
6.4: I am bigger than my thoughts	79	At times when you are focused on unhelpful thoughts.	
6.5: Stepping off the hamster wheel back into reality	80	At times when you are focused on unhelpful thoughts.	

Part

3

Uncovering our emotions

In the following section of this book, we are going to look specifically at our emotions. Sometimes, emotions can be tricky little blighters and, often, they are a bit uncomfortable. Sometimes, by pushing away our negative emotions and chasing after the positive ones, we miss out on what is right in front of us and miss out on fully living our lives. Through waking up to the reality of difficult and sometimes painful emotions, you will discover a fantastic sense of relief, clarity, productivity and well-being. In this section, you will also learn:

- to notice your busyness, whatever you are doing;
- to understand that you do not need to 'run away' from difficult emotions, and that running away can make life a whole lot more difficult;
- to find ways of understanding what lies beneath your busyness;
- how to accept difficult emotions as part of life;
- that managing emotions with mindfulness releases lots of energy, productivity and mental clarity to help us to get ahead in life;
- to recognise that you can continue to be busy and increase your effectiveness, efficiency and sense of ease when mindful of your difficult emotions;
- to let go of fantasising about positive feelings and, instead, focus your energies on being grateful, being kind and being playful as ways to improve your well-being.

The painful truth

When we unhook ourselves from troublesome thoughts, when we stop trying to think positively and stop distracting our busy minds in other ways, what do we find? What are we *really* avoiding and trying to get away from? What is all this busy rushing around in aid of? What is our purpose with it? When we take a look, by stepping out of our busy thinking mind, allowing it to slow naturally, to still or recede, then up pop the emotions.

Usually, when emotions sneak in, we tend to respond to them habitually and reactively, often in a way that is not too helpful for us. Through a practice of noticing our emotions, we can become more familiar with them and understand them better, which is the most important step to figuring out what to do with them when they show up. We will come on to that later but, first, let us jump straight in to a super quick mindfulness practice that you can use anywhere at any time.

Practice 7.1: Mindfulness right now!

What am I feeling?

▶ Notice and name how you are feeling emotionally right now (feelings tend to be described in one word, such as: happy, excited, bored, frustrated, angry, sad, anxious, stressed), e.g. 'Here is a feeling of boredom.' If you are not too sure what is there, perhaps noticing whether the feeling is pleasant, neutral or unpleasant.

▶ Acknowledge the fact that you are noticing your emotions.

▶ Notice how you know you are feeling this emotion. Where in your body does this emotion show up (lightness in the heart, tightness in the chest, butterflies in the stomach)?

▶ Point to the area of your body where this emotion feels the strongest. If you notice that it is all over your body or you cannot locate a specific area, then just point to an area in your body at random, perhaps to the middle of your body or the heart area.

▶ There it is, that emotion, and then there is you, acknowledging it – nothing more than that.

As you go about your busy days, continue to practise noticing your emotions (the 'good' and the 'bad' ones) and acknowledge the fact that you are noticing them, in the way described above. You may notice how you feel when you:

▶ speak to your colleague at work, partner at home, etc;

▶ rush around walking from here to there;

▶ catch sight of a stunning cherry tree from the window of the bus as the drivers change shifts;

▶ hear the water boiling in the kettle as you make a quick cup of tea;

▶ are sitting at your desk at work.

Our wired world

Initially, recognising our painful emotions can be tricky, as every cell in our bodies goes on 'red alert'. As you will recall from Part 2, our cortisol levels rise (we feel we are under threat), we feel stressed by trying so hard to figure out just what to 'do' about it all to make it stop and go away. We bump into our difficult emotions and try to 'fix' them, preferably really quickly, because they do not feel nice, both physically and mentally. The more we keep going and struggling like this, the worse the feelings get, until often we end up giving up.

We see this in our clinic every day. The case example below highlights such an instance. Rita, perhaps just like you, struggled with the counter-intuitive idea that, if we just stop trying so hard to fix everything, then life becomes much simpler and we are much more effective. The strength of this pattern nearly led her to quit therapy (like so many other things she had tried so hard with but still felt like she was 'failing'). Instead, she realised that there was nothing to fail, because this was not a test, an appraisal or a kind of trick – there was not really anything at all to fix, figure out or mend.

Rita

Rita was an attractive, successful and intelligent young woman who worked as a management consultant in the city. She had always worked diligently and unceasingly to overcome her 'flaws' and manage her 'deficits'. She did this at work, in her relationships and even questioned the very core of her personality. She came to therapy seeking another answer to her problems, looking for strategies and techniques to cure her depressed mood and persistent feelings of failure. Her expectation for dealing with her difficult emotions was to look at what therapy could do about them, to get rid of them and she was prepared to work very hard to make them go away.

➤

She took out her notebook to write out her to-do list from the session and found the explanation that this was not going to work quite shocking.

This is an excerpt from a session, discussing her difficult emotion of loneliness. She is asked to do nothing about it, just to breathe mindfully, to notice her thoughts and physical sensations arising. It went something like this:

Breathing in: tension in the solar plexus.

Breathing out: overwhelmed with feeling of loneliness.

Breathing in: *this is unbearable; I have to make it stop.*

Breathing out: tightness in the chest.

Breathing in: feelings of panic.

Breathing out: *I can't do this.*

Breathing in: *I need to make it stop.*

She stops the exercise, exclaiming she cannot do mindfulness. She is crying. She is encouraged that she has got it! But she does not understand. She is absolutely right; she cannot 'do' mindfulness. She has just discovered her habitual pattern, the one that is the real cause of so much distress. She is noticing all those thoughts exclaiming to her that she 'cannot cope' and she is believing them, and wanting desperately to act on them by 'doing' something. Because this response to her difficult emotions is so habitual for her and she is such a high achiever, she has attributed her success to her busyness and her failure to not trying hard enough.

This has meant Rita has become busier and tried harder, even when it has not been working. Consequently, her performance at work declined, she was depressed, anxious and working longer and longer hours with no time for her relationship, friends or pleasure. In fact, when Rita learned that she could be just as busy without grasping at success and running away from failure, her anxiety and depression left, she had a successful relationship, felt happier and became more productive, confident and efficient at work.

Emotions are a condition of life, not a problem to solve

We live in a society that is geared towards a medicalised view of our bodies and health. If we experience sadness or anxiety, or any uncomfortable physical manifestation of these emotions, we assume that these are a problem and that they need fixing straight away. Our thinking mind pipes up, we start to evaluate our experience, judge it and analyse it, we take ourselves off to the doctor and say, *Look, I am anxious, my heart is beating fast,* or *I am sad, I can't get the energy back to get out of my bed, what's wrong with me?* Our minds overanalyse, they go into problem-solving mode and focus on these experiences as *the problem,* but they are not.

Sadness, anxiety, anger, guilt, shame, boredom, grief and discomfort, and all the physical manifestations of these, are all part of what makes us human. It would be unusual never to have experienced these feelings and sensations at many different times in our life. Of course, they are unpleasant and we do not want them around when they show up, but often they can provide us with important information, if only we listen to them. Emotional pain, just like physical pain, has a purpose – it is an evolutionary response. Emotions are not the problem.

It is our attempt to suppress, control and eradicate painful feelings via our endless attempts to think through them, avoid them and solve them and the inherent struggle in this respect that is our real problem. Struggling with our feelings is the problem. Do not take our word for it. Have a go right now, reflecting on your own experience of trying to push away, fight or fix your feelings.

You will notice that this next exercise is similar to the one in Chapter 3, called 'How is busyness working for me?' We think that there is great value in revisiting this concept time and time again. Noticing the function of our behaviours and whether those behaviours are serving us well or not can be extremely helpful in attempting to better manage our demanding and busy lives.

Practice 7.2: Mindfulness right now!

Do what works (in the long term!)

▶ Make a list of all the strategies you have tried in order to resolve difficult feelings. Here is a list of common ones we regularly encounter in our clinical practice to help you get started; checking/adding to/completing to-do lists, working overtime, drinking alcohol/caffeine, taking drugs, avoiding socialising, thinking positively, problem-solving, using social media/your mobile phone/playing games to distract yourself, worrying, arguing, people pleasing, comfort eating, reading this book!

▶ How do these strategies immediately help you/are they effective in the short term (e.g. feel better, avoid some difficult feelings, feel like you are getting somewhere – probably)?

> ▶ Do any of these strategies permanently get rid of these feelings (probably not)? Do any of them increase your difficult feelings in the long term (we guess sometimes they might)?

> ▶ And, if you use these strategies regularly in the long term, are there any costs to your health, well-being, relationships, self-confidence, quality of life, missed opportunities, sense of busyness?

> ▶ How effective are these strategies in moving you closer to the aspects of your life that you care most about (e.g. your improved relationships, mental and physical health, productivity, sense of accomplishment)?

Of course, some of these strategies might be helpful (reading this book, we hope), so keep doing what works for you. However, we are guessing that you probably use some strategies that can make things worse in the long term and take you further away from the kind of life that you would prefer to be living or the sort of person you would prefer to be, and it is these exact strategies and not your feelings, therefore, that are the real problem.

Busy bee

Have you ever seen someone flailing their arms and legs at the mere sight of a bee? The bee triggers a surge of panic and they try everything to get the bee to go away. The more they try to bat the bee away, the more it frustrates the bee and increases the likelihood of the bee staying close by and that person getting stung. Maybe that person is you? It is the same for our emotions: the more we try to bat our unwanted emotions away, the more unwilling we are to have them around. Perhaps, by staying as busy as we can possibly be, the more likely they are to linger around, increase in their intensity and cause a painful sting on our lives.

The best thing to do when a bee is around, is to stay still, watch it for a little bit and perhaps step aside if needs be or open a window for it to fly away when it is ready to. Similarly, the antidote for all of our struggling with our difficult emotions is the opposite of struggle, it is about letting go of the struggle – letting go of all the over-thinking, problem-solving, rushing around and trying to push away our 'pain' and, instead, be willing for these emotions to be around until they are ready to dissipate in their own good time. We do not need to like them or want them to be around, we just need to be willing to have them, to accept them. In other words, *acceptance of what is,* and that is what mindfulness is all about. Using mindfulness to manage difficult emotions is not about feeling better, but about getting better at feeling whatever emotion is showing up, in any given moment.

When practising acceptance of emotions, it is best to practise when it is a little easier, when the emotion is not too overwhelming, and work your way up. For this next exercise, you might find it helpful to bring to mind something that has left you feeling a little distressed, perhaps a dilemma at work, a small quarrel with a friend or a difficult decision you have to make.

Practice 7.3: Mindfulness right now!

Turning towards our emotions

▶ Begin by sitting in a comfortable and balanced position. Tune in to your breathing to anchor you in this present moment.

▶ Bring to mind a situation that is mildly distressing for you. Let your mind think freely about this problem for a short while.

▶ Next, expand your awareness throughout your body and notice what is here right now. Notice what emotions are here and their sensory qualities, perhaps tightness, heaviness, discomfort somewhere in your body.

▶ Gently guide your awareness to an area of the body where you feel discomfort more vividly. Be curious to what this really feels like, in this place in your body, right now.

▶ Gently stay with the discomfort and explore it in more detail, notice the intensity of it, where the discomfort starts and where it finishes, perhaps drawing a mental outline around the sensation, noticing how much space it takes up in your body. Getting a sense of whether it is moving or still, hot or cold, sharp or dull, towards the surface of the body or deep within.

▶ Allowing your experience to unfold moment by moment, letting go of any urges to try to change your discomfort. Breathing alongside these sensations.

▶ If you notice any thoughts that distract your attention, see if you can notice these and allow space for these too and guide your attention gently back to the tangible sensations of discomfort in the body.

▶ If it feels OK to do so, and as you breathe alongside your discomfort, silently say to yourself, 'I know this hurts and I can be with it.'

▶ If the sensations become too intense, turn your attention back to your breath. When you are ready again, return the attention back to the discomfort. Come back to the breath and end the exercise whenever feels right for you.

What will we do when nothing we do will do?

What do we do when we feel busy and overwhelmed? Well, most of us keep *doing*, making plans and new to-do lists, prioritising tasks and doing more – in the hope of getting everything done and making all the stress and 'pain' go away.

What do we tend to do when we feel difficult emotions, discomfort and pain? Well, we usually tend to avoid it, try to get rid of it and keep *busy* to distract ourselves.

A lot of our busyness and associated stress and anxiety to get things done on the surface is a lot more to do with escaping the feelings that are lurking underneath, rather than what we think it is all about – so much to do, things to get done, people to please, success and happiness to get!

With most of the busy people that come to see us for therapy, it is often the case that their busyness is all about trying to get rid of painful and uncomfortable feelings of some type or another. Whether they are busy with work, the children, socialising, trying to find a partner, or all the above, when we drill down with them to find out what would happen if they just stopped, let go of any urges to keep all this busyness going, they invariably all admit to feeling scared that, if they simply stopped all this *doing* and all that keeps them busy, they would feel worthless and then vulnerable!

Now, worthlessness and vulnerability are just words, terms that many of our clients seem to use, along with others like, *not good enough, a failure, rejected, alone, unlovable* – they are just terms that we are now using to describe this painful experience that lurks beneath our busyness, you can call it what you want, any term will do, even 'X'! Remember, feelings of worthlessness and vulnerability are very scary to us *all*, we have internalised a prehistoric message from our ancient ancestors that these feelings are connected to our downfall, in other words:

Worthlessness/Vulnerability = Death/The End

It is not at all surprising, therefore, that we would all struggle with these feelings, that we would try our best to avoid, escape or hide them from ourselves or others.

How often have we stopped to think what would really happen if we just let go and did not rush around *doing* all the time?

▶ How devastating would it really be?

▶ What really is the very worst thing that would happen?

▶ Would our world really come to an almighty sudden crash and traumatic ending?

Well, the reality is no, of course it would not! All we are trying to avoid is our own feelings, our vulnerability and imperfections. Some of us know this and still fear that once all this is exposed and revealed to ourselves and/or possibly to others – then our world will end, but nothing is the end of the world except the end of the world – these are just feelings after all and you will not die, your world will not end simply as a result of you experiencing all this. The feelings that you may be trying to run from are part of you, part of the human experience for all of us – we are all in the same boat here. You cannot run from them and you cannot hide, so it will be helpful for you to learn to sit with them or you will just get more stressed and busier trying not to!

Try to invite all your experience in – it is kinder to yourself when you find a way into your life experience instead of desperately trying to find a way out of it all the time. The very fact that we are terrified of experiencing a part of us is telling us what is most important to us, what we want and need more of, which is often a greater sense of safety and security that we can give directly to ourselves with more self-directed attention, care, compassion and connectedness (in other words, mindfulness).

So, next time you feel rushed off your feet, busier than the busiest bee in town, try the following practice, which comes in two parts.

Practice 7.4: Mindfulness right now!

What is underneath my busyness?

Part 1: Drilling down

Ask yourself the following questions:

▶ If I *do not* act on this urge right now (e.g. to go out, work on this project, check and answer emails, check my Twitter and Facebook messages, call a friend, boss, mother), what am I really concerned might happen?

▶ And what is the problem with that/what might happen then?

▶ And what is the problem with that/what might happen then?

▶ And what is the problem with that?. . . For example, I will feel 'X' (worthless, failure, rejection, unlovable, vulnerable).

Part 2: Stop stirring the pond

▶ Right, so there it is, your 'X' (e.g. feelings of worthlessness/vulnerability) with all the busyness, stress, anxiety and frustration whirling around it.

▶ Now for a few minutes, just sit observing this experience and any feelings of anxiety, frustration, busyness and stress.

▶ Let these feelings come and go as they will naturally. Notice the urges to act on these feelings or any urges to take the feelings away. Notice how the intensity of these feelings and urges change.

▶ Notice any thoughts that arise, maybe about how this is not helpful, you have too much to do, there is not enough time in the day for this mindfulness lark! Allow these thoughts to come and go as if they are passing clouds in the sky of your awareness.

▶ Now focus in on one of the most intense feelings you have, maybe a feeling of worthlessness, vulnerability or associated fear, anxiety, sadness, general stress or frustration. Locate that feeling in your body; is it in your chest, stomach, head, shoulders, heart, legs? If you feel it all over your body, then hold your whole body in your awareness.

▶ Hold this feeling of pain in your awareness, like a caring parent will hold a crying child, give it your time and attention right now. You do not have to like it, just hold it.

▶ Now breathe into the area of your body where this feeling resides, imagine your in breath flowing around this feeling. As you breathe out, let go of all struggle and tension you may have with this feeling, imagine your out breath carrying this struggle away.

▶ Again, breathe into and around this feeling. And, as you breathe out, let go of all struggle and tension you may have with this feeling.

▶ Allow this feeling to be here just as it is, allowing the breath to create space around it.

▶ The feeling may change or it may not. Remember, the goal is not to change the feeling but to accept it, it is part of you, it makes you human, we all experience it, let it be.

Time to SLOW down

Mucking about and struggling with difficult emotions tends to create more of them, not fewer. We get frustrated that we are still feeling anxious; we are anxious about our anger, we are bored with always being anxious, depressed about always feeling stressed. This is time-consuming and inefficient. This gets in the way of us reaching our targets and goals and living the life we would prefer. This is certainly, therefore, the moment to SLOW down. We mentioned this acronym back in Chapter 4, but here it is again to help remind us what we can do when we meet difficulties, feel overwhelmed and at our wits' end:

S Stop whatever you are doing and bring your awareness to your breathing.

L Let thoughts, opinions, judgments and urges be.

O Open up your heart, body and mind to what you are feeling.

W Where is most important for you to put your attention right now? (For example taking care of yourself, being present with friends/family, resting the mind, finishing off important work.)

When SLOWing down in this way, your attention might settle on the feeling itself for some time. You may find that you are able to bear this feeling after all or perhaps discover that it was not as bad as you imagined it might be. It is possible that it might even give you some clues as to what might be most helpful to do.

This is life, Jim . . .

You may like to kid yourself that you are a Vulcan like Spock and are ever so logical. Emotions do not come into the equation of a busy life or making quick rational decisions and your 'feelings' simply are not compatible with good business, performance, success and staying on top of your game. This is a fun idea, perhaps, and quite nice for the next Star Trek convention, but it simply is not true. Whoever told you this was possibly misinformed –it is all a trick! You are human (really). You may not like it, sometimes it basically sucks, but there you have it. Here is another nice science bit to help you get the message that emotions are really, honestly, very, very important and, yes, you do have them.

As psychologists, we recognise that emotional pain often is rooted in early childhood experiences. The human brain is not born fully developed, so early experiences are highly significant in shaping our brain function, neurology and biochemical responses to stress. Think nice, round blob of Play-Doh.

Now we understand that cognitions (our thinking minds) are dependent on emotions – as Sue Gerhardt (psychotherapist) points out: 'Cognitive processes elaborate emotional processes but could not exist without them.' In essence, our higher brain function, such as making sense of our emotions through our thought processes, develops later than our basic 'old brain'. So, as tiny babies, we can express basic physiological needs through crying, etc. But we are totally dependent on our experiences – such as physical contact, care and nurturing – from an adult to meet those needs and then to help our brains to develop. Think of making a gentle dent into the Play-Doh with your thumb.

If our needs are not met, or met poorly, we suffer. At the most primal levels this is akin to feeling like we are going to die. This is as dramatic as it sounds because we are absolutely helpless as infants, we also do not have the developed higher levels of cortical (brain) functioning to understand or make sense of the situation. Think fist splatting Play-Doh into a pancake.

This brain functioning does develop, but it takes several years, hence children go through differing levels of comprehension – including the egotistical age of two, not believing in the tooth fairy any more (your parents were liars) and painting your room black as a misunderstood teen. You probably, recognise some or all of these stages, but together they make a tower of different coloured blobs and splats of Play-Doh.

So, the quality of the relationship between an adult and the child profoundly influences brain structure and biochemistry. If this process lacks sensitivity, then our cognitive development is impaired, we do not understand our emotions and we do not experience ways to regulate them; our levels of physiological arousal, associated with emotion are easily either aggravated or suppressed. Splat the whole tower.

The good news is that, even as an adult, we can create new and improved neurological pathway and can learn to regulate our emotions. We need to work hard to establish these by practising again and again, but this will also get easier and easier to do. Roll the Play-Doh into a cool giant rainbow blob or any other shape you like.

We can then SLOW down. We recognise our physiological arousal, we let ourselves experience it and thus do not repeat or reinforce our habitual response, and we 'let go' through non-attachment and bring our attention and energy to somewhere more helpful, offering ourselves up a nice new neurological pathway. We can skilfully and gently adapt from the most stressful situations this way, from past childhood distresses to present-day concerns. In mindfulness, we learn that, rather than trying to control our emotions (push them away, try to fix them), we can develop a fresh new relationship with them, one of acceptance and turning towards our emotions, which generally is more helpful in living life to the full.

Turning towards our emotions and letting them be

=

Less stress

=

Better mental and physical health

=

Greater effectiveness and moving towards a meaningful and fulfilling life; the life you want.

Respond from the center of the hurricane, rather than reacting from the chaos of the storm.

George Mumford, author of *The Mindful Athlete*

Mindfulness top tips to-go

In this chapter, you have learned that it is helpful to do the following:

▶ Identify and acknowledge your emotions (the good and the bad).

▶ Stop trying to figure out or get rid of emotions, as this will only stress you out more and make you busier and inefficient.

▶ Discover what vulnerable feelings lurk beneath and motivate your busy behaviour and urges.

▶ Stop trying to avoid your deeper vulnerabilities and imperfections; you are human after all.

▶ Find a way into your life, rather than out of it; let all your emotional experiences in.

▶ Hold your painful emotions in your awareness, let go of struggling with them, breathe alongside them, open up around them and make space for them.

Falling gracefully

How come we are so keen to reduce and avoid certain feelings like anxiety, frustration, anger, sadness, loneliness and grief, while feelings like joy, excitement, happiness and calm are ones we want more and more of? This may seem like an obvious question, but take a moment to think about it right now, as all of these feelings are completely natural and essential to being human.

We tend to label our feelings as 'positive and negative' or 'good and bad' because of how physiologically they feel in our bodies. The 'negative' stuff tends to create tension, tightness and exhaustion in the body, while the 'positive' stuff tends to create lightness, warmth, fuzziness and spaciousness. Any of these emotions, however, can be a helpful clue to what we have or do not have in our life and what we want or need. We will come back to this idea later in this chapter but, for now, let us consider the reason for all the unpleasantness in our lives and how we might approach falling in to the pits of these emotions in a more graceful fashion.

Safety first

Many of the feelings we do not like, that are uncomfortable, are the ones designed to keep us safe. When noticing a threat, we jump straight in to fight, flight or freeze mode, whether we like it or not. We might feel sensations in our body that we call anxiety, panic or fear that prepare our body to escape a threatening situation quickly, while anger serves to push people and other situations away that we may perceive to be harmful to us. All this discomfort that we experience in our body is like a warning signal, telling our body to do whatever it takes to keep us safe and protected from harm.

This safety mechanism is extremely effective, to the extent that it can get signalled even when there is no real threat there at all – it can simply be imagined in our minds (as we discussed in Part 2 of this book). The problem then arises when we become so fixated on our anxiety-related concerns, especially in our busy, hectic lives, that not only do we lose our ability to discriminate effectively between what is real and what is imagined, but we are so pumped full of anxiety (and many of the other unwanted emotions) that we become fearful of even taking time to reflect on what is going on. Act now, think about it never.

What can happen often, as we have seen, is that these primitive caveman/cavewoman tendencies trigger a lot of adrenaline, which – especially when over-used – clouds our thinking and leads to unhelpful decision making, not to mention lots of physical aches and pains, which all impede our progress with what we want to achieve in life. All this panicking, stressing and trying to sort it all out *right now* is quite inefficient and tends to shrink our world. We know that many of us feel like we thrive on a certain level of stress, we feel alive and energised. This is exactly the point of adrenaline – it is stimulating, but only for relatively short periods, before we end up burnt out. Many psychological studies have shown that certain levels of anxiety and stress impair concentration needed for decision making and reduce the quality of our work and performance in life more generally.

Putting on the brakes

By noticing, acknowledging and turning towards this discomfort, we are putting the brakes on our autopilot mind. Instead of jumping to our automatic, natural reactions, we can SLOW down enough to decide a different route that may take us in a much more helpful direction. Take a look at this next case example to see how it can be helpful to put on the brakes when our emotions are running high.

Ellen

Ellen had a wide circle of friends and spent much of her time outside of her working day visiting them, hosting elaborate dinner parties and keeping up with all their birthdays and anniversaries by buying gifts and baking cakes. When friends visited, she would ensure the house was spotless, filled with fresh flowers and would spend several hours preparing food. She admitted that it was difficult to keep up with all of this on top of her work and taking care of her children, but she kept going in this way as she dreaded the idea of her friends being disappointed if she didn't make the effort.

In fact, therapy helped Ellen to recognise that underneath all her busyness she was afraid of being rejected by her friends and ending up alone and lonely. At one of her therapy sessions, Ellen explained that she had become very upset as a friend had not thanked her for all her efforts after a dinner party. When this type of thing would happen in the past, Ellen found herself quickly feeling angry and either messaging her friend to say how upset she was and that she wasn't welcome around again or she would stonewall them and ignore them, allocating them to her 'black book' as she called it. Unfortunately, this often resulted in arguments with her friend, leaving Ellen feeling increasingly distressed.

➤

However, on this occasion Ellen was able to remind herself of the SLOW down technique. She acknowledged that she was feeling angry and upset, and realised that her feelings were a sign of just how important her friends were to her. She decided instead to message her friend to say she had a lovely evening, appreciated her coming along and asked whether she enjoyed herself. Her friend replied thanking her for all the fun they had and invited her around for the next gathering. Over time, Ellen also came to realise that she didn't need to make so much effort trying to please her friends as it was her company they enjoyed and not whether the house was spotless and the food perfect.

When it all just gets too much

Sometimes, our feelings can be so overwhelming it is hard to get perspective as easily as Ellen did. Sometimes, our anxiety might lead to a panic attack, our anger turn to rage or we might just feel completely disconnected from what is happening around us. Of course, if these feelings are a sign you are in real danger, get yourself to a place of safety and call for help, if necessary. Once you are safe, then try out the following exercise to bring you back to the here and now.

Practice 8.1: I haven't got time for this!

Loosening the grip

▶ Acknowledge how you are feeling right now, perhaps saying in your own mind, 'I am noticing that I am feeling anxious/angry/sad.'

▶ Notice where in your body you experience these feelings most vividly.

▶ Notice that you are breathing and how you are breathing, whether ragged, short, fast, shallow, painful, whatever it is, just as it is.

▶ You do not need to fix your feelings, push them away or ignore them. Whatever happens, the feelings will not last, nothing does.

▶ Remember that you have not always felt like this, you will not always feel like this, this is a moment of distress.

▶ Now notice where you are indoors/outdoors. Notice what you can see around you – people, objects, lights, colours.

▶ And notice your feelings, just as they are, no need to change anything at all.

▶ Now notice what you can hear: traffic, birds, ticking of a clock, hum of electricity and notice that here, too, are your feelings, just as they are.

▶ And focus on your breath, noticing the natural rhythm and flow as you let go of the grip on your feelings. Letting them be just as they are.

▶ If you are able to practise like this, keep going. Keep returning to the breath, no matter how often or how strongly you are distracted by thoughts or feelings.

▶ Watch the feelings changing all by themselves, in their own good time.

Papering over the cracks

For many of us, sticking to the same routines and schedules day in and day out can become rather mundane and thrill-zapping. Add to this the little time that our busy lives allow for fun and frolics, being so busy can be a real drag most of the time. We might try to do more, engage in more just to paper over any possible boredom lurking beneath. This becomes a tiresome effort as the cracks just keep appearing. When we practise mindfulness, the paper is peeled away and often we find boredom underneath.

Yet boredom and distraction are often just the first layer in emotion, masking over something else. Usually, they serve a purpose as strategies for avoiding something, such as even *more* uncomfortable feelings like impatience, fear, sadness or grief. Already, boredom is giving us a helpful clue that we are avoiding something, that we feel uncomfortable and we want it to go away.

Mindfulness can become a fertile ground for boredom as we learn to stay with the urge to avoid. This can be done by adopting an attitude of curiosity . . . oh, look, I am bored to tears, how very interesting! Perhaps we can let go, allow our habitual thoughts and urges to 'do something about it' just to pass, to dissolve, which can be a lot less exhausting and stressful than constantly trying to fight it away. But then, back comes our habitual mind, sometimes as quick as a flash and, each time we do this, we push away our life, we reject our true feelings, we reject ourselves. Probably, we are traipsing down one of those old familiar neural pathways. As soon as we avoid the present moment, here and now, we start to increase a sense of dissatisfaction and the urge to get away from it rapidly to doing something (another to-do list, perhaps? Or how about reformatting that spreadsheet?). We perpetuate our boredom and dissatisfaction with life, ironically, we increase our pain, our busyness and layer it over with an illusion (like finding something else to do). But when we are mindful of our emotions, often we recognise what we are up to, what we have been avoiding and papering over and, in this case, it is boredom.

There are so many ways to paper over our emotions, keep up the pretence, just watch the ads on TV – perhaps a new shampoo will be the answer to your woes? No, then try a new car? A great rate of interest on that mortgage? A trip abroad? The possibilities are endless. More distractions, more opportunities to avoid boredom, two for the price of one; more ways to perpetuate your dissatisfaction with life each more promising than the last. It is not your fault, life is full of fascinating ideas, objects and sensations – perhaps we have just forgotten that *we*, too, are one of those – right here, right now. How about pulling back that paper and finding the door and walking on out into the fresh air? Go on!

Practice 8.2: Mindfulness right now!

Booooring!

▶ Notice how you know you feel bored. Perhaps if there is something specially 'bored' about your posture, your facial expression, your breathing or thoughts.

▶ How bored are you? Rate from 0–100 per cent.

▶ What urges do you have to paper over your boredom:

(Choose any): food, TV, Twitter, Facebook, talking, drinking, texting, sex, magazines, exercise, work, radio, DIY, helping others, drugs, drawing, smoking, cleaning, worrying, holidays, gambling, daydreaming, driving fast, bird-watching, clubbing, plate-spinning, inventing, sleeping.

▶ Remind yourself of the Zen saying: 'If you understand, things are just as they are. If you do not understand, things are still just as they are.'

▶ Try holding these thoughts/feelings/sensations with gentleness.

▶ Let go of habits to cover up boredom and watch boredom unfold. It is only an experience, only sensations, only a moment.

Each time you let go of your struggle with this emotion you are letting go of a lifetime's habitual way of thinking and responding to it – just one breath at a time.

Deep impact

When we begin to become more aware of what is lurking underneath the papered walls, we might also notice what effect it has on our body. If you were to scowl all day long, the chances are that you would feel more stressed and frustrated as a result:

Try it right now.

▶ Scrunch up, wrinkle and contract your brow, hold it . . . hold it . . . and notice how you feel emotionally as a result, in this very moment . . .

What happened? Did you feel instantly more p'd off? The chances are you did. Similarly, if you tense your stomach muscles or clench your jaw, you may feel more agitated and stressed. Go on, give it a go now, gently. So, make a purposeful effort to check in with your facial expression and bodily tension, as often as you can, and you may find that you are able to notice changes to your emotions and sense of busyness by some simple body awareness and realignment.

Practice 8.3: Mindfulness right now!

Settling in comfortably

▶ Notice your body posture as you are sitting or standing. Are your shoulders hunched up, your back arched over? Readjust so your shoulders drop, your back straightens and you are in a comfortable and balanced position.

▶ Become aware of the muscles in your face and where feels tight or scrunched up. See if you can loosen your jaw, smooth your forehead, widen your eyes.

▶ Scan your body for any areas that feel tight or restricted. Breathe in to and around this place in your body, letting go of any tension as you breathe out.

▶ As you continue to breathe, imagine air filling your stomach as you breathe in and pull your tummy button towards your back as you breathe out. This will help to slow down and deepen your breathing.

Sad case

Boys are not supposed to feel sad. Girls are, but only if they do not wear mascara. Sadness often gets pretty squashed. Anger is a bit more acceptable, especially in public, and it looks cooler, but take a closer look and there is probably sadness, too. And, so, we might see that we have been trying, or are trying to turn our sadness into something else: anger, confusion or helplessness. It is uncomfortable.

Sadness needs a lot of care, but we will never access this while we are harsh, critical or blameful towards ourselves or others, no – sadness will hide away. 'Phew!' you might think, it is best avoided – let us stick with the macho stuff, please. But we know your secret (and ours) – this is the soft spot; this sadness is our Achilles' heel, our 'weakness', we have found the Kryptonite! We guess yours is something like, 'I am not good enough, I can't cope, I am stupid, no one wants me, I am crazy', which all equals 'I am unlovable.' So, your secret is that you think no one will/should/could love you.

By just paying some mindful attention to our pain, to our sense of vulnerability and being unlovable, we can find that it is quite bearable (and even loveable). Well, that is what Meera discovered, as you can see in the following example.

Meera

Meera: (crying) Who would want me? Look at me. I am so sad and broken.

Psychologist: Have I told you the story of the broken pots?

Meera: What?

Psychologist: OK, so it goes a bit like this. Every day a lady goes to the well to fetch the water. It is a long walk and she carries two pots on a heavy yoke across her shoulders. One pot is whole, the other is cracked. The cracked pot is sad, as it notices how hard the lady works and how it is letting her down by not holding the water. It says to her one day, 'Please throw me away, I am no good, I am broken.'

➤

The lady says, 'But, sweet pot, you bring me such joy, have you not noticed how the flowers bloom along your side of the road?'

Meera: Are you calling me a crack-pot? (laughs)

Psychologist: Yes, and that is so precious. You are human and I recognise that, I know what that means. With your tears, I see your vulnerability and it touches me. Look at me now, leaning forward towards you in the chair. I am engaged. I feel connected.

Meera: But that is just you.

Psychologist: OK, so there you go again. It does not matter if I love you or not or if I am connected to you or not, if you cannot accept yourself as you are. So, no wonder you feel so lonely. Are you rejecting yourself because you do not feel whole? You expect someone else to want you when you do not even want yourself. Even if they did want you, why would you trust that if you do not believe you deserve to be loved? It leaves you feeling so isolated and alone and unloved. Just like now, here . . .

Meera: But . . . I do want to be loved.

Psychologist: Yes, that is not the problem, is it?

Meera: No. I want to be loved for being a whole pot, but I am not. I am broken and I want to be fixed.

Psychologist: And you are not fixed.

Meera: No. I do not want to be sad.

Psychologist: I know, and you are. Let us just sit with that for a moment and breathe.

With mindfulness, we give the sadness some attention; we name it and notice it, we recognise it. We see the brokenness and vulnerability, which we have spent so long racing away from and busying ourselves along with a 'just get on with it' attitude. We notice the way we have rejected our pain, denied it while we jump into tasks and chores. But now see that, just by giving ourselves some simple attention, a cup of tea (and – go on – a biscuit, too), so to speak, we can bear this experience of heartache, longing, loneliness, helplessness and sense of our unlovableness, and with this attention we offer love. And then we can let this go, we can allow it to pass as it inevitably will. And do you know what the great paradox is? It is your misery, your suffering, sadness and vulnerability; your great fear of being unlovable that makes you so loveable.

It's good to cry!

Another thing you might notice when you begin to turn towards your sadness is that you might cry. Interestingly, our tears serve a helpful function by helping to manage our sadness. A study was conducted to look closely at the physical properties of tears. They compared tears from cutting onions, tears of laughter and emotional tears, such as grief. When they looked at these different types of tears under a microscope, they found that they all looked vastly different. Different types of tears are made up of different molecules. Our emotional tears contain a neurotransmitter called leucine encephalin, which is a natural painkiller that is released when we are feeling stressed. If you have ever given yourself the opportunity to have a good cry, you may have experienced a sense of relief and, perhaps, even felt better for it, and this is why.

Grief and loss

Grief is the melancholic of our guests. Sadness cloaks this one. When grief strikes us suddenly and unexpectedly, it is a shock and, even when she sneaks up, seen in the shadows of long illness or old age, we can find her familiar face still catches us unaware. We can also grieve for lost opportunities, lost youth, money or possessions. Every day, in our busy lives, we might notice our losses, even in little ways with not enough time for this or that or some regret: the too tight trousers, the mouldy yoghurt at the back of the fridge, the missed calls, missed lunch breaks and rapidly passed weekends.

Some everyday losses can feel even greater: the missing out on that bonus and work promotion or even the loss of our jobs that we had poured so much of ourselves into. Then the winter comes, leaves fall from the trees, friends, family, lovers come and go. Sadness can pervade our lives as we see this endless cycle, particularly when we come into contact with a significant loss.

This following is a piece of a story about someone in a state of shock and grief and their use of mindfulness at that time. This is what she wrote.

Lucy's story

My best friend's boyfriend has just been killed in a sudden and tragic accident. She has just texted me, telling me she is on the way to the hospital with his parents to

➤

---

identify the body. She described this as a 'living hell'. There is nothing to say, nothing to make this one change, to 'make it better' or turn back the clocks with 'if only' or 'why'. When death comes like this, there are no more chances to say, 'I love you' or to resolve the wounds of our past; a life is simply swept away, leaving behind a great gaping hole of grief. As a friend, all I can do is to be there. This too is the role of mindfulness. I hold the aching form of my sorrow with tenderness and let myself crack. There is no correct way to 'behave', I am numb, angry, disappointed, despairing or quietly sad by turns, sometimes none of these. No choice but to ride this wave.

Try the following exercise whenever you like, paying attention and offering acceptance to your loss and grief. No matter how small or large this sadness feels, try this exercise to acknowledge and be alongside this sadness.

Practice 8.4: I haven't got time for this!

Reflective mindfulness

▶ Give yourself a quiet space to sit in stillness.

▶ Allow the grief to come, as it may, in waves.

▶ Open up to this washing over you, as you also open your heart to this suffering that connects all living beings.

▶ Keep returning to your breathing to ground you in the present, in your life, here and now, just as it is.

▶ It may be helpful to remind ourselves 'this too shall pass'. Allowing emotions to come, letting them go as you gently still the mind.

It can be a jarring experience, when we meet with grief, that the world continues on. The earth continues to turn on its axis, the sun rises, people continue with their activities, there is still washing up to do, etc. However, it is also these activities, this continued rhythm of life, that can help to bring us back again. So, while we need to take time to accept our grief with tenderness, we also need, eventually, to begin to find our contact point for re-entry into life. We need to recall that spring inevitably will follow winter, that we can re-engage and that there is still joy to be found. This can take a lot of time (that is fine) and it can be accompanied by guilt and doubt. Just like other practices in mindfulness, we can return to our point of contact with the present, our point of engagement with life, over and over again.

Below is an extract about a father whose 16-year-old son died suddenly in a tragic gun accident. He describes the place of mindfulness in his grieving.

> During the day, I observe a variety of thoughts. 'I can't do this anymore . . . my life isn't worth living; I failed as a parent'. . . All the while I attempt patiently to return to my breath. I forget, and return. I go away with my thoughts and return. I notice my impatience, and return. I see now that underneath the thoughts and the emotions, underneath the sorrow, the emptiness and all my grief there is something else. It is the absolute unconditional love that I have for a beautiful young man whom I simply miss very much.

> In Myla and Jon Kabat-Zinn, *Everyday Blessings: The Inner Work of Mindful Parenting, pp. 347–8*

Good grief

When we see the pain, distress and agony of loss, it may be that we discover something more, something that tells us about our purpose, our deep connection to others, to our planet or to our commitment to ourselves. For example, the ending of a relationship can be very painful and, yet, perhaps if we seek deeply, we may also find our fragile and loving desire to care for others and to be cared for, too, we may find our deep wish to be well, to be happy and to feel safe. Then, alongside the pain of this loss, we also see what is most important to us, our true heart, one that longs to connect, one that misses or has missed that chance with this person, or that part of our life, and knows the pain of it. This desire is bigger than death or endings, because we continue to mourn the loss of connection, despite the absolute inevitability of it. In other words, we all seek, desire and need human contact, attention and care and yet all of us will one day die, all the relationships we have will cease or change.

Grief is the emotion that reminds us of our connection to others, that reminds us that, even with these fragile feet of clay, we have an infinite capacity to love. To love and to lose are two sides of the same coin; one cannot be experienced without the experience of the other.

A word of caution – watch yourself if you find you begin to use mindfulness as a way to avoid life. The notion that mindfulness practice can be a way to be immune, aloof, cut off or removed from grief is misguided. It really is a form of denial, stuckness and arrogance, telling us that we are 'above' this need for contact with others, this 'neediness', somehow superior to it. We may tell ourselves that loss is 'the will of God' or that 'life is just a dream', or it was 'meant to be' – such platitudes delude us that we can hold such pain at bay. Seen in others, they can be, frankly, humourless and beyond the pale.

Mindfulness top tips to-go

In this chapter, you have learned that it is helpful to:

▶ Look at the effects that our difficult emotions have on our body and how they affect our thinking.

▶ Realise that our difficult emotions often serve to protect us and that avoiding them often only serves as a waste of time and adds further stress to our lives.

▶ Notice that boredom and distraction often tell us that we are avoiding something, some uncomfortable feeling that we would like to get rid of.

▶ Recognise that difficult emotions are part of our lives in an infinite number of ways and we can and do cope with them – and this is amazing in itself.

▶ Acknowledge difficult emotions and see them as part of being human and being alive.

▶ Notice that these emotions, no matter how painful, often tell us what is so important to us, what we need and desire as human beings.

▶ Realise that you *can* continue to use mindfulness when these or any other difficult emotions arise.

9

Letting the good times roll

If only we'd stop trying to be happy we could have a pretty good time.

Edith Wharton

When we are so busy and hectic, certainly it can feel like there is no time in the day to feel anything good. We are talking about all those lovely, warm and fuzzy feelings like love, excitement, joy, peace, calm and gratitude, to name just a few. As we explored in the previous chapters, if we are constantly trying to keep uncomfortable feelings at bay, in the hope that we will reach everlasting happiness, we tend to find that this leaves very little room to savour any sweetness.

The more that we attempt to push away anything that is uncomfortable, unwittingly, we push away feeling good at the same time and can end up in a state of numbness. Just like an anaesthetic, we do not feel anything painful, but it means we feel very little of anything at all. And this anaesthetic is only temporary as, sooner or later, the pain returns, so we then keep having to take more and more anaesthetic to keep the pain away. As we continue to rely on all this anaesthetic, how truly awake and alive are we, really, to our lived experience? Along with the increasing feelings of low mood and anxiety that arise when we maintain these ways of being, another fact is certain: we seem unaware and almost oblivious to other experiences in our lives. We miss out on any meaningful experiences in life that would, no doubt, give us satisfaction in abundance.

Attack of the sleeping zombies!

Much of the time, it is as if we are blundering through life 'asleep', absent from most of what goes on in our lives, absorbed in primitive fear, much akin to a population of zombies! It is important that we wake up and show up to our lives, as they will continue to tick away, whether we are present and connected to them or not. We can assure you that, with the transformative power of mindfulness, you will be showing up to your life more often, reaping and enjoying the varied and numerous rich fruits it has to offer you.

Strangely, it can be a real challenge, especially in our Western, busy lives, to allow ourselves any genuine pleasure. As we have seen, many of us spend a lot of time uneasy, 'looking over our shoulders' or second-guessing the next dilemma in a defensive position, readying ourselves to deal with and solve the next problem that arises to avoid any further painful feelings. If pleasure can even penetrate this fog of anxiety, often we do not even really know how to savour it, and instead already mourn the time when it will be gone or worry about grasping it a bit harder and thus end up squeezing all the life out of these fleeting moments of joy and tumble back into a miserable downward spiral.

Maybe you even find yourself shuddering at the idea of feeling anything pleasurable. Perhaps your mind is thinking you do not deserve all this good stuff, especially as you have not done enough yet, you need to do more cleaning, more work, more helping others out, more organising for the following week, more of anything and everything and then you can sit down and ahhhhhh . . . relax. But by that time, you probably find yourself exhausted and irritable, worrying about all the other things you have got to do later. And maybe nothing you do is ever enough and you will never deserve to feel good, and all this positive stuff is to be avoided at all costs.

Finding ease with life's ups and downs

Grim stuff, all this. So, here is the good news . . . letting go and accepting life in a state of ease and openness is not a very common experience for many of us, and yet it is a very natural state for us to be in and we love it. You may find that, by dropping the judging or evaluating of the worthiness of something (e.g. job, relationship, your body, yourself in general), then your experience of life becomes more and more about just being there in the moment, and that can bring a great sense of ease to your life, whatever else is going on.

When we recognise painful emotions and see them as a fundamental (and natural) part of life, we see that it is pointless (in fact impossible) and ineffective to fight or flee from them. The truth is that you cannot pick and choose which emotions you want – you can try, but our guess is that, if you have attempted this, it has not been that helpful and has not made for an easy ride. Because of this realisation, we are free to experience a deep kind of relaxation, even alongside our difficulties. This is both mentally and physiologically healthy, as many studies into mindfulness have now shown.

Further studies into mindfulness, specifically related to kindness, gratitude and developing compassion, show that enhancing these can also improve our health, well-being and level of functioning. Also, research has shown that these qualities occur *because* we accept our difficult emotions and our vulnerabilities and not despite them. It is this very quality of acceptance and, perhaps even more so, willingness to accept life as it is that leads us, ultimately, to being free from unease. When we are at ease, we experience a fundamental sense of well-being; we feel joy, contentment and peace in our hearts. This is not a giddy, grasping euphoria where everyday life seems bland and mundane by comparison. This is the realisation that the bland and mundane are nothing of the sort, that what appears ordinary is rich, sweet and delicious (it is also part of the deal, it is part of our life). We then know that all that muck that we have been in is this fantastic fertiliser for all this great rosy stuff to come springing up out of.

> The tiny seed knew that in order to grow, it needed to be dropped in the dirt, covered in darkness, and struggle to reach the light.

Sandra Kings

The crazy paradoxical thing about this is that, without pain, we would not know pleasure and it is only our own mind discriminating one from the other anyway. Take Marmite, love it, hate it, whatever. Marmite is just extremely salty black stuff (or so our very own extensive scientific investigations have shown), whether you like it and it gives you pleasure or you hate it and it gives you pain is totally subjective. This is the same for anything.

Practice 9.1: Mindfulness right now!

Yin-yang, thank you mam

Have a go at thinking through the answers to the questions below:

- ▶ Do you say pot-ate-toe or pot-art-toe?
- ▶ Is the cup half empty or half full?
- ▶ Is this a picture of an old lady looking down or a young lady looking away?

▶ Are you on the top of the world or on the world's bottom?

▶ What is the sound of one hand clapping?

▶ Was your mother always right?

▶ If so, who was left?

▶ Is the answer to this question yes or no?

We know, stupid quiz, you might say, and we would agree, but add that it does illustrate that all these questions and concerns about good, bad, right, wrong, nice or not nice can bog us down and we can get carried away in trying to figure it all out instead of just rolling about in life with a willingness to savour all it has to offer as each new moment unfolds. This is, essentially, joyful, like a puppy rolling about in the grass.

To help you along with this we have another handy acronym. This time it is EASE:

E Embrace: everything, nothing more, nothing less, all experiences.

A Accept: just this moment, this experience as it is.

S Soften: no need to interfere, struggle, work it out or evaluate it, let it be.

E Exhale: you can keep breathing (notice how, when you are tense, full of anticipation or struggling with effort, often you hold your breath and this can increase physical and mental 'up-tightness'; when we exhale, naturally we relax slightly and let go).

When we come to appreciate our reality – that life is 'just this', and only in those moments, do we realise that we can make SLOW choices, because we are freed from our habits, caveman/woman tendencies and knee-jerk reactions. As Carl Rogers, a famous psychologist, once aptly said: 'The curious paradox is that when I accept myself just as I am, then I can change.'

The overview effect

This reality of ours is a lot more incredible than we tend to realise. For astronauts, they have really had the best opportunity to get a physically wider perspective on the world. When in outer space looking back at the earth, often they describe a profound experience, a shift in their thinking and sense of self-awareness. From this place, they have, quite literally, stepped back from their usual day-to-day activities and gained a new viewpoint with a completely fresh perspective, which they call *the overview effect*. From this new perspective, they report a deep sense of awe at the fragility of earth, the complexity and beauty of nature, the ebb and the flow of weather, the impermanence of life and the realisation that earth is just a drop in a vast expanse.

In mindfulness, we too can get a sense of this effect. By practising stepping back from our thoughts, our feelings and the rest of our experiences, we too can gain a fresh perspective and see the bigger picture. Just like the astronauts, we can discover what really matters and where we really want to put our time, energy and attention. We also learn to appreciate the beauty in little moments of our life, the beauty of the sun shining on our face or freshness of rain, the impressive design and technology of our gadgets, the comfort of our sofa, the smell of fresh coffee and the tastes of our food.

Try out the next exercise to see if you too can experience a similar shift in perspective to astronauts, but without needing even to step out of the front door, let alone travel to outer space.

Practice 9.2: I haven't got time for this!

The sound of music

▶ Find a song on any of the many devices on which you can play music or search online if you have not got a song freely available.

▶ Get yourself in to a comfortable place where you are able to give your attention to the music.

▶ Press play and bring your attention to the sounds of the piece.

▶ Notice any sensations in your ears and become aware of the volume, rhythm and tone of the music.

▶ Notice what instruments are playing. Bring your attention to one of these instruments and follow the sounds it makes with your full awareness.

▶ If, at any moment, your mind wanders to thoughts, other sounds, sensations in your body, that is OK See if you can acknowledge where the attention has gone and gently guide it back to the sensations of sound.

▶ Now expand your awareness to the full breadth of all the sounds that make up this song and any emotions or energy that are conjured up as you take the time to appreciate the music.

▶ Take a moment to consider all that has been involved in creating this experience for you right here right now. The training of the musicians, the creativity and expertise in producing this piece along with the technology that has been developed to be able to share this song. Allow any thoughts and feelings to drop in to your awareness.

▶ As the song ends, bring your awareness to your breathing and thank your mind for this experience. You may also wish to thank all that was involved in giving you the opportunity to listen to this music.

Gratitude

When we are so busy bustling along in our lives, we can forget gratitude easily. Often, we often overlook all those chances to be pleased with our lot. This is especially true if it is 'one of *those* days'. The dog ate our breakfast, we missed the bus, the boss is in a bad mood and, no matter how much we think of stardust, it just is not cutting it. What is there to be thankful for in this? What about being met with a hot, steaming helping of illness, bereavement, redundancy, assault, eviction, bankruptcy or other threats to our safety or well-being?

This would be a good moment to reach habitually for the choccy biccies. Give the following exercise a go to enhance your awareness of gratitude.

Practice 9.3: I haven't got time for this!

Biscuit bountiful

▶ Hold the biscuit in your hand and see it, just this moment.

▶ You have this very biscuit to chomp (or crisp, or whatever morsel usually takes your fancy) just as it is.

▶ Notice your anticipation of eating.

▶ Take a bite.

▶ Just let it sit in your mouth for a moment before it disappears.

▶ Feel the taste seeping into your mouth; allow it to permeate your senses.

▶ Savour the changes in taste and texture as you chew.

▶ Feel the sensations as you swallow.

▶ What are you eating, disappointment? A sense of lack? Pleasure? Gratitude? Or something else?

Research suggests that practising gratitude is one of the most reliable ways of increasing feelings of happiness. This can be enhanced by making a daily record, perhaps in a diary or on your phone or tablet, of things for which you feel grateful. This really helps to develop the 'attitude of gratitude'. This can include absolutely anything you like – from being thankful for having clean water to drink to recalling the kindness of the person making your coffee (that might be yourself). If you are having a grumpy moment, it might be handy to look at a previous list to inspire you, and then you can add your gratitude now for having done this task (and maybe even for waking up to your grumpiness).

The gift of giving

A simple act of kindness can bring you great personal rewards. There's nothing quite like the gift of giving. When you see first-hand the impact it can have, it becomes the best feeling in the world.

Richard Branson

It is painful to see others not taking care of themselves and, if we know this, we also know that when we do not care for ourselves, we hurt others too. When we are too busy to notice this, often we are blind to the careless-ness with which we treat others. We can get caught in a 'who's had the hardest day' competition with our partners or bury our head in a book, pretending not to see the pregnant lady hanging on bravely to the rail in the bus, we walk hurriedly past the collection tins, *Big Issue* seller and lost tourists.

But do you remember a time when someone showed you a random act of kindness? Maybe they gave up their seat for you, offered you a helping hand, gave you a spare ticket to something, a thoughtful gift or made a friendly comment? Many of these gestures cost us very little in terms of time or money and yet they can make such a significant impact on our day, or even our whole life. As psychologists, we know the precious value that even the simple act of listening to someone can have, even in the direst of circumstances.

If you think you do not have time for expressing gratitude, kindness and appreciation, try this following exercise as you go about your days and see how it goes.

Practice 9.4: I haven't got time for this!

Cheers, nice one!

▶ Make a commitment to say 'thank you' at every opportunity.

▶ Try to drop sarcasm and any insincerity. Recognise this instead as an aspect of possible anger that needs some acceptance and attention all of its own (return to the previous chapter to refresh on how to manage your anger mindfully).

▶ See if you can say 'thank you' with more than just the obligatory passing phrase. Can you really connect with genuine feelings of gratitude? If so, you will sound different – go ahead and try it.

▶ You can enhance this exercise by really looking at someone and saying, 'Thank you. I really appreciate what you have done,' 'Thank you. I'm very grateful for this/that,' or 'Thank you. Doing/saying x was very kind of you.'

In the times in which we live, simple actions such as a smile or a 'thank you' go a long way. They are usually manageable, even when we feel tired, rushed off our feet and/or downright miserable. If you want to crack the icy layer of frost lying over your frozen sense of joy, verve and interest in life, then this exercise can be a really good and easy place to start.

When we guide our attention away from our stress-inducing busy stories and worry in the mind, we are cutting off the fuel that keeps them going. Our attention can then turn to putting ourselves truly in the minds of others and we can offer our understanding and care. By committing to random acts of kindness, even for small moments in our day, we can really increase our sense of peace and reduce our stress.

Practice 9.5: I haven't got time for this!

Random acts of kindness

These can be grand gestures or small ones, it does not matter. Here are some ideas. Use these or your own. Start by picking three, do them today or as soon as you can and when you are willing:

▶ Water the plants, feed the cat, play with the children, phone greatauntie Hilda, have a bath, go to the gym, look out of the window for a moment and enjoy the view, listen to some music, complete an unfinished task, leave a task unfinished, give to charity, send someone a cheery text message, buy a gift for yourself or for someone else, clear away the clutter in your home, tidy up, leave a mess, put on some fancy clothes, take them off (woo-hoo!), make love, make tea, take a break, let someone else take a break, etc.

▶ You may also like to crack a smile or make friendly (not flirty) eye contact with a passer-by on the street, maybe saying 'good morning' or the like, simply acknowledging their existence.

Simple actions, such as a nod or smile, can have a profound impact on how we and others feel (in a good way). It is actually quite amazing to notice how many of us are looking down, avoiding eye contact as we rush around, perhaps totally absorbed in our screens. No wonder we feel so isolated, cut off and alone a lot of the time. Are we scared to let others in, to leave ourselves exposed? What are we hiding? If you want to feel more alive, connected and joyful in life, committing to doing these random acts of kindness, weekly or daily, can work a treat (we highly recommend them).

Take a look at the example below to see how such simple acts of kindness can really be quite life-changing and also help us to realise what is important to us in life.

Alf

Alf was a very successful broker who had been through two difficult divorces. He found that he was at a juncture in life where he had suddenly lost all his confidence, was unsure of his current relationship and his work and questioned what the point of it all was. Despite his wealth and success, he felt something was 'missing'.

Every day, he passed a homeless man (we will call him Ed) on his way to the office. Come rain or come shine, there Ed was, wrapped in a tatty old blanket, with his dog on a string. Alf started to nod to Ed and sometimes say 'hello'. Occasionally, he chucked over a bit of spare change. Then, one day, after considering the wisdom of giving money to someone who might use it to buy drugs, and not wanting to be party to this, he bought Ed a cup of coffee. From then on, Alf started to say 'Hi, how are you doing?' and have a brief chat. One day Ed replied, 'Oh I'm OK, it's my birthday today'. On a whim, Alf decided to get him a card. He gave it to Ed, and Ed's eyes filled with tears; he told Alf that this was the first card he had had in 13 years.

Alf was profoundly affected by this interaction. He began to recognise these very such small acts of kindness occurring in abundance all around him. He realised he rarely smiled, said 'thank you' or appreciated even the small things in life. He began to understand what he had been missing.

Child's play

As children, most of us loved simple pleasures. You may recall lying in the grass and watching the clouds, building dams in streams, playing football with your friends, collecting stones or stickers, skipping and running – just for fun, care-free. You might even remember times when you saw or did things for the first time, your first look under a rock, the first time you learned to ride a bike or your first kiss.

Life can be like this now, when we open those innocent big eyes of ours (no matter what you have seen before) and look at the playground we have in front of us. As adults, most of us even get the big toys and games to play with – like cars, real money and sex. We can make decisions and choices about where and when we go and with whom. And, sometimes, especially when we are having a tough day, we might like to remind ourselves how to play by going to a comedy show, watching a children's film, eating chocolate by torchlight under the duvet, buying sweets or blowing bubbles in the park.

Practice 9.6: Mindfulness right now!

What kind of playful person are you?

▶ What did you enjoy playing as a child? Did you play mostly by your-self, with friends or pets? What helped you really to feel free, embracing the moment? What made you laugh out loud or giggle?

▶ What things are you already doing in your life as an adult that give you a similar feeling of playfulness? Perhaps you enjoy exploring new places, laughing with friends, playing computer games, competing at sports just for fun?

▶ Is there anything you have wanted to do, that you just have not had the time to try out, but you imagine that might be fun or give you a sense of joy? Maybe doing some colouring, going for a walk with no place to go, going to a concert or watching a scary movie?

▶ Notice if any emotions show up, whatever is here is welcome. It is possible that even imagining playful times can bring about a sense of warmth around your heart.

Studies have shown that bringing playfulness in to our lives and acting like a big kid can really have a profound impact on our well-being. Do not take our word for it, try it for yourself. Next time you see a tall tree, what about giving it a climb? Or rolling down a big hill till you get dizzy? It might feel a bit odd at first but, if you really surrender yourself to having fun, you may find feeling good starting to wash over you. Otherwise, while freeing yourself up from worry and your busy stories, we advocate putting some time in to your day to do whatever you find good fun.

Most of us assume that happiness comes to us from the world around us (that is what we have been led to believe), but stop searching and striving for this to appear magically and come your way; happiness and meaning is already inside us all, it is down to our own way of being – it is up to us to create the reality we want for ourselves.

> When people come to the end of their life and look back, the questions that they most often ask are not usually: 'How much is in my bank account?', 'How many books did I write?' or 'What did I build?' You find the questions such a person asks are very simple: 'Did I love well?', 'Did I live fully?', 'Did I learn to let go?'
>
> Jack Kornfield

Too much of a good thing

How many times have you longed for your weekend or holiday to begin, only to find that once it has begun you are not enjoying it as much as you had anticipated, feeling anxious as you count down the days, minutes until its inevitable end and you are right back at work? What about feeling sad and alone being single, anxious that you will never meet anyone and longing for a partner to take that pain away, only to find that once a relationship is under way, you are scared and worried that your partner may leave you or that the 'grass may be greener' with someone else?

Clinging hard to positive emotional states that come from events, such as weekends, holidays or being in a relationship, while simultaneously remaining fearful and averse to negative feelings, such as those associated with going back to work, being single or 'stuck' with a partner who annoys you, is human and understandable, but often results in an emotional rollercoaster effect in life.

The truth is that our emotions change, as do our life circumstances, so having a strong attachment to a situation or event, and the inherent positive feeling that comes with it, is going to result in frustration and disappointment every time, leading to soaring highs and plummeting lows in your mood.

Take a look at Jackie in the following example. She clung to positive experiences and struggled with negative ones – ultimately, these ways of being caused much upset for her and brought about the exact reality that she feared and wanted to avoid.

Waking up and letting go of our natural tendency of attachment to positive feelings as well as our aversion to our negative ones means that we may come to experience more:

▶ emotional stability and balance in our busy life;

▶ clarity of mind to get ahead and move on to the things that are important to us;

▶ of the reality we want for ourselves.

If we are unable to do this, we may find ourselves feeling a bit 'sick of the ride' (pass the bucket, please).

Jackie

Jackie felt that if only she had a partner then her life would be 'perfect'. She had a career as a successful litigator in a reputable city law firm, she had friends (who were all in relationships themselves), a home and a close relationship with her parents, but no family of her own. She longed to be in a relationship and felt very sad and low in mood the more she ruminated on the fact that she was 'alone' and single. She became increasingly anxious that she would never meet a partner and, instead, live life as a spinster with her cat.

When Jackie finally met someone through an internet dating website, her mood rocketed sky high, she was elated and ecstatic and it was not long (about one week, to be precise) until her thoughts turned to fantasies about the picturesque future of this relationship. She began to imagine and secretly plan her wedding, looking into reception venues and possible honeymoon destinations. She decided, at this time, that all her problems were over and that she no longer needed to attend any further therapy sessions.

It was about four weeks later when Jackie telephoned again to make another appointment. Sure enough, the relationship had not worked out and she explained that her now ex-partner had found her too clingy and preoccupied with worry that the relationship might come to an end. She was beside herself with grief and sadness.

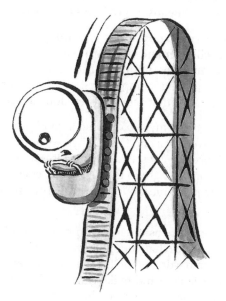

Fantasising and dreaming

Perhaps, like all of us, you think that, if life was just a bit different in some ways (less busy and hectic, smaller nose, bigger house, better sex, promotion, less rain, stronger body, honest politicians, etc.) *then* we could be OK, we could at least find our way, maybe sustain it and *enjoy* life a bit. Fantasies and dreams can look innocent enough, and often are. However, they can also be the poisoned chalice that taints our world by promising 'real happiness' and leaving us dissatisfied with our lot.

When we begin to crave past experiences, alternative realities or a perfect future, we are inadvertently rejecting the present and ourselves along with it. By looking for something else, something a bit better, more of a 'good' time, we are also saying 'this is not good enough'. That might even be true sometimes, and then we have acceptance, but change the emotional tone to one of perpetual dissatisfaction and we see the repetitiveness, the undermining of anything pleasant or 'positive' anyway, and we just want more.

Imagine going on a date, being dressed in your glad-rags and sitting down for some scintillating conversation over a miniature plate of expensive morsels. Your date is not looking at you, not talking to you and not even picking at the food. Instead, they are constantly looking over your shoulder, scanning the room, checking their phone, fidgeting and, no matter what you do, your date just is not interested. This is you.

When you fantasise constantly about something better, this is what you are doing to yourself, over and over. Just a bit depressing, is it not? Not only that, but this can get harmful, too. The fantasy can be inflated further through gambling, dieting, compulsive behaviours, promiscuity, drug-taking or just about any other activity when done to excess.

So, we have exploded the myth of 'having a good time' because, when it gets like this, it is 'avoiding a bad time'. When we notice this, we are undoing all that avoidance, we are seeing life as it is. We see, hopefully with a little grace, that we are sat right in the muck and, guess what? That person over there laughing just a bit too loud is probably up to their eyeballs in it, too.

Try this following exercise as often as you can as you bustle about your busy existence and notice that you might be engaged in unhelpful habits such as fantasising or daydreaming. It is a great and very quick way to help you wake up and feel alive and make contact with your life – your rich, present moment experience, whatever that may be.

Practice 9.7: I haven't got time for this!

Sense-sational

▶ Stop, right now, whatever you are doing (maybe reading this book), wherever you are.

▶ Look up and around you.

▶ Take a breath.

▶ Invite all of yourself in.

▶ Awaken from the dream.

▶ Notice the colours, hear the sounds, smell the scents, touch the textures and savour the taste of your life right now. This is it.

Repeat the above whenever you become aware of fantasising or acting in unhelpful fantasy-prompted behaviours. See if you notice the realisation occurring that, even if you have a strong desire to escape reality, you do not *need* to act on this. You can arrive at this moment here and now and allow the sense of freedom and relief to arise and rush into this moment, which comes along with letting go.

Mindfulness top tips to-go

In this chapter, you have learned that it is helpful to:

▶ Notice that everlasting happiness is an illusion, despite what we are told, so stop chasing it.

▶ Allow negative emotions in to our lives as it can create more space for positive ones too.

▶ Be more at EASE.

▶ Recognise that grabbing at positive emotions and pushing away negative ones preoccupies our attention and uses up energy and prevents us getting ahead in life; we remain asleep to the beauty of the world around us and the sense of satisfaction within us.

▶ Step back from our hectic minds, allowing a different perspective to emerge, one where we begin to notice all that sweet stuff we have been missing out on.

▶ Be grateful, commit to random acts of kindness and be playful to improve our well-being, reduce stress and live life to the full.

▶ Let go of fantasies and the pursuit of positive feelings and instead focus on what is here right now – the good and the not so good – it is all part of life's richness.

Tracking your practice

Part 3 has seen an abundance of different mindfulness practices. Remember, the intention is not to do everything all at once, the intention is to begin slowly incorporating mindfulness practice in to your life, in a way that works for you. Of course, we are not forgetting all the exercises you have learnt so far and covered in Parts 1 and 2. Instead, return to these whenever you like. It might even be the case that you continue trying out the practices from the previous parts of this book before you start practising the ones from this part. There is no right or wrong way to practise mindfulness.

With the following practices, we encourage you to make a note of which ones you have found more helpful and that you would like to try out again at another time.

Practice	Page	When?	Notes
7.1: What am I feeling?	88	As often as possible, perhaps when you notice a sudden shift in how you feel.	
7.3: Turning towards our emotions	93	When you feel distressed and experience difficult emotions.	
8.1: Loosening the grip	104	When you are feeling overwhelmed by your emotions.	
8.2: Booooring!	106	When boredom shows up, e.g. on the bus or waiting in a queue. When you feel slowed down and less busy.	
8.3: Settling in comfortably	107	At regular intervals in the day, such as when you go to sit down at your desk, on your travels on the train, just before a meeting.	
8.4: Reflective mindfulness	111	Whenever it might feel helpful to give space to feelings of loss and grief.	

Practice	Page	When?	Notes
9.2: The sound of music	121	When listening to music When you feel grumpy and/or ungrateful.	
9.3: Biscuit bountiful	122	You can try this whenever you eat snacks or at mealtimes.	
9.4: Cheers, nice one!	123	Throughout the day, as often as possible.	
9.5: Random acts of kindness	124	Try doing between one and three a day, or at least one per week.	
9.7: Sense-sational	130	As often as you can, when engaging in unhelpful habits, if you find yourself fantasising. How about doing it right now?	

Part

4

Taking care of me

Isn't it ironic that the one person we expect so much from is the very person that often we give the least attention to. When we neglect ourselves, it becomes so much more difficult to manage and successfully meander our way through our busy and hectic lives.

In this next part of the book we are going to explore:

▶ How we tend to treat ourselves and what affect this has on our well-being and functioning as we go about our busy lives.

▶ The benefit of self-kindness and how it is a skill that we can cultivate.

▶ Ways of being loving and compassionate to ourselves as an antidote to self-criticism.

▶ How to handle difficult relationships in our lives.

▶ Practising self-care to build resilience to stress and busyness.

10

Cultivating
self-compassion

The losing game

Do you find you often compare yourself to other people? Perhaps you find yourself looking at the enviable figures of celebrities, comparing your achievements to your colleagues, scrolling through social media and noticing what wonderful lives all your 'friends' have while you deem yourself less worthy, feeling dissatisfied, sad and stressed. You may notice that this can lead to the expectations that you place on yourself forever increasing. On the one hand, you may argue that these high expectations provide you with goals to aim for, motivating you to improve yourself and better your overall quality of life. However, you may also notice that, more often than not, you fail to meet these high expectations and then you are left feeling like a failure, hopeless and fed up with it all, caught up in a perpetual cycle of busyness and dissatisfaction.

As we explored in the previous chapters, we can also hold unrealistic expectations that we must avoid difficult situations and any associated uncomfortable feelings at all costs. As this is impossible to achieve for any significant length of time, sooner or later we lose out and then begin to blame ourselves and others around us for not meeting our demands; fuelling anger, low mood, shame and a whole host of other unwanted emotions, often the very ones we were trying so desperately to avoid in the first place.

Kirstin Neff, a researcher in the area of self-compassion, writes:

> Striving to achieve and setting high standards for yourself can be a pro-ductive and healthy trait. But when your entire sense of self-worth is based on being productive and successful, when failure is simply not allowed, then striving to achieve becomes tyrannical. And counterpro-ductive. Research indicates that perfectionists are at much greater risk for eating disorders, anxiety, depression, and a whole host of other psy-chological problems.
>
> *Self-Compassion,* pp. 70–1

If any of this is sounding familiar, we would encourage you to give the next practice a go.

Practice 10.1: Mindfulness right now!

Constant demands

Spend a few moments reflecting on these questions and become aware of the thoughts and feelings that arise.

▶ Finish these sentences with the first thing that comes in to your mind:

I should always . . .
I must never . . .
I have to . . .
I am so . . .
Other people should not . . .
It is unfair that . . .
No one ever. . . .
I always . . .
I am never . . .
Nothing is . . .
I am not . . . enough

▶ What feelings show up when you make a mistake? (disappointment, shame, humiliation, fear, guilt, failure?)

▶ What do you tend to say to yourself when you make a mistake or notice a flaw, what language do you use and how is your tone of voice?

▶ How do you treat yourself when you have not managed to achieve all that you set out for yourself, or you have failed in some way? Do you berate and bully yourself or are you understanding and kind to yourself?

▶ What do you deny yourself to avoid failing in the future? What needs do you ignore to make sure you get everything done (food, water, relaxation, sleep, love)?

▶ What are the consequences of treating yourself so harshly?

▶ When you realise you have not achieved what you wanted, do you tend to rush to fix this or do you give yourself time for care and self-kindness?

▶ Who and what do you compare yourself with?

▶ When is ever good enough?

▶ Are you criticising yourself now as you recognise you are lacking in self-kindness?

Take a moment to stop and notice what showed up for you during that practice. If you are berating yourself about the answers, stop right there. There is no benefit from beating yourself up for beating yourself up!

The truth is that it is really hard to be human, living in a busy world that has such high expectations of us, that is so competitive and that fears failure. It is not your fault if you tend to view the world in this way – if you also fear failure and how you, others and the world are just 'not being good enough'. Often, we hear messages that we are lazy when we stop to care for ourselves, that we are never good enough and that we need to change so much of ourselves just to fit in. However, have you ever stopped to think about what impact all this criticism has on our well-being, confidence and functioning in life? How does all this affect our sense of busyness? Perhaps it is time to treat ourselves more kindly.

Kicking the dog when it's down

As we have seen, we are wired in a way that means we persist in trying to solve problems in our lives, yet the real problem arises when we view our unpleasant emotions as problems. This is understandable, as these emotions tend to feel bad and we attempt to eradicate them in any number of ways. One way we do that is by beating ourselves up for even having them – telling ourselves that we should stop it, just get over it, pull ourselves together, perhaps, even, that we are weak, pathetic and stupid for ever feeling this way in the first place. This is the message that many of us have heard from people around us, even our very own loved ones when we were growing up. It makes sense that we would tell ourselves off for feeling these ways, if we have been led to believe that it is wrong.

Self-criticism in this respect is, therefore, functioning to protect us, to better us and trying to make us feel better. However, this harsh self-criticism generally does not help, in the longer term anyway. In fact, often it makes us feel worse. When this critical mind is left unchecked and it is pervasive, it continues to chip away at our confidence and can lead to a whole host of psychological problems.

When you are suffering, you do not need criticism, you need kindness. After all, if anybody else on the planet had your unique DNA, your unique childhood, your unique life history, your unique physical body, they would respond in exactly the same way that you respond. This is something that Helen realised when she came for therapy. The following is an extract of the conversation where she began to realise how she had been treating herself after becoming upset at work.

Like Helen, you might notice that you have treated yourself like this for a really long time and it is hard to know anything different. Perhaps it might even be difficult to consider giving up your self-criticism? Perhaps you are reluctant to

---

Helen

Helen: I just don't know what's wrong with me, I get upset so quickly and easily. There's clearly something wrong with me that I'm never going to be able to change. I'm so pathetic that I let such a small issue affect me so much.

Psychologist: Can I ask you to just pause for a moment. Take a deep breath.

Helen: (Takes a deep breath)

Psychologist: What do you notice your mind saying right now?

Helen: I'm thinking I'm abnormal and weak.

Psychologist: Ouch! And what feelings are showing up right now as your mind judges you like that?

Helen: It's horrible. I just feel worse.

Psychologist: Is this familiar? Having your mind beat you up like this when you are upset?

Helen: Yeah, I do it all the time.

Psychologist: And does it always leave you feeling worse?

Helen: Yeah it does . . . (pauses) You know what, it's like that phrase 'kicking the dog when it's down.' I've been doing that to myself, haven't I?

Psychologist: I guess you have. If you buy into those thoughts, then that's what you've been doing, yes. What do you think the dog really needs? Does it need to keep being kicked or is there something else?

Helen: I guess it really needs to be protected, taken somewhere safe and looked after.

Psychologist: Is that the same for your feelings? Do they need to be protected and given some care?

Helen: I guess so, I just don't know how . . .

---

stop listening to this part of you because you are worried it will mean you will get nothing done, that you will not be as successful as you are or could become, that you will not be as good a friend, partner or worker. That makes a lot of sense because it is likely that it has helped you to be where you are today and achieve all that you have, to some degree, but it does not bode well for your well-being, confidence and achieving all that you might want to in life.

This self-criticism often leaves us feeling on edge, anxious, angry and exhausted. When we feel these ways, we are not in the best psychological state to get things done, in the best way we can. In fact, we might even put things off until we feel more confident, more motivated or calmer, which would be quite understandable and what many of us tend to do. We might also put things off because we fear them going wrong and we know that when that happens our critical mind will continue to tell us how it is all our fault and we failed. Have a go at the next practice to think about this some more.

Practice 10.2: Mindfulness right now!

Two teachers

▶ Imagine someone you care deeply about. Bring them to mind and notice any sensations that may emerge around your heart.

▶ Imagine that this person is learning a new, challenging skill. Perhaps learning to drive, to play the piano, a new language.

▶ Now imagine that there are two teachers, teaching your loved one this skill. The first is a harsh critical teacher. When your loved one makes a mistake, they shout at them, 'No, no, no! What have you done?! What's wrong with you? You are always making mistakes; you are so useless at this! You're pathetic!'

▶ What impact would this have on the way your loved one felt? Their performance at learning this new skill? Their motivation to carry on?

▶ The second teacher understands how difficult it is to learn this skill. They calmly say things to encourage your loved one to keep going like, 'Nice effort. Keep it going. This is really hard. that's not quite right, what about trying this?'

▶ What impact would this approach have on the way your loved one felt? Their performance at learning this new skill? Their motivation to carry on?

▶ Which one of those two teachers would you want your loved one to have?

▶ Which teacher are you more likely to hear in your own head as you go about your busy life?

What if we told you that, instead of beating yourself with a stick, there is, in fact, an alternative to this harsh critical self that can help motivate, support, protect and encourage you, helping you to get things done and manage your way through your busy life? What if we also told you that this alternative had all the benefits of self-criticism yet did not come with any of the negative drawbacks that you get from beating yourself up? And, that it was, in fact, necessary for your survival. The truth is that, although most of us have lost touch with, and become unpractised in this alternative approach, it is, in fact, deeply wired into our brain systems and particular ways of being, which are all older than our species itself. If you are anything like us, we bet you would be keen to hear more. Well, first, this alternative is called, *self-compassion.*

Self-compassion

As we have seen, at the heart of mindfulness is awareness. Inherent in this is acceptance. As we embrace and accept the nature of both our own private experience (thoughts, feelings, behaviour and sensations) and the busy world around us, we begin also to allow life simply to unfold.

Compassion is a quality that arises naturally from our clarity and acceptance. When we observe how we and those we love (as well as those we do not, or those we feel quite neutral about) suffer from being caught in their struggle to accept reality, then we can look into the very heart of suffering with a kind of fearlessness. When we understand pain, and suffering without grasping for something different, nicer or 'better', then we see the very truth and reality of life. We see that we all suffer – from the smallest beetle to a great blue whale, the wealthiest rock star to the poorest street urchin. Without exception, each creature is subject to ageing, illness and death – at the very least. This realisation, while it can be quite painful, also liberates compassion. And now, instead of avoiding pain, using mindfulness, we accept the reality of it and, alongside this, are then able to offer genuine, authentic empathy and care to ourselves and others.

Self-compassion can be defined as a sensitivity to our own suffering and a motivation to help alleviate and prevent it. It is all about acknowledging when we are suffering, and then purposefully responding to that suffering with genuine kindness. By leaning in towards our difficulties with courage, non-judgement and understanding, we can ease our suffering and develop resilience. We can also learn to be gentle and warm towards ourselves when we suffer and come into contact with our vulnerability. Through self-compassion, we shift perspective on our pain and suffering. Rather than seeing this as a threat, becoming single-minded and rigid in a state of fight or flight, attempting to escape and eradicate it at all costs, we calm, regain clarity of mind, become psychologically flexible and behaviourally effective, allowing us to move towards what matters most to us once again. In this state of ease, our perspective is expansive, we see more than the so-called threat of suffering, allowing us instead to meet our suffering with a genuine warmth, spaciousness and care. When we are suffering, being kind to ourselves is in fact essential in order to move towards what truly matters to us in our life. We function at our best when we feel valued, loved and cared for. Perhaps it's time to therefore be kinder and more caring towards ourselves.

All in the same boat

When we are not able to meet our expectations or we make mistakes, we may feel very alone as if no one else suffers. Self-compassion helps us to recognise that all human beings suffer because we are all imperfect and vulnerable. When we are suffering with a sense of failure or any other emotional pain, we can learn to recognise that this is something we all go through, that we all share this in common. Self-compassion involves the recognition of this shared common humanity. The truth is that we all mess up. We all let down people who we know and love. We all struggle with painful thoughts and feelings. Busy or not, we are all very much in the same boat.

Cultivating self-compassion

You might or might not be surprised to know that the way that we breathe is, in fact, very much connected to our emotions. When we feel anxious, panicky or angry, our sympathetic nervous system is activated, leading our breathing rate to increase and become shallower. By focusing our attention on slowing down our breathing, we activate the parasympathetic nervous system, slowing down the body and mind, helping to soften our emotion, making space for mindful awareness and a more helpful response to our emotions. When we are suffering in some way, experiencing painful feelings like anger, anxiety and sadness, acknowledging this and attempting to alleviate some of the distress is an act of self-compassion. By activating our self-compassionate minds, we become better able to tolerate and make space for challenging emotions. Give this a try now and feel free to use this technique before any of the other exercises you engage in over the course of the book.

Practice 10.3: I haven't got time for this!

Soothing rhythm breathing

▶ Find a comfortable position where you are upright with your feet flat on the floor.

▶ Close your eyes, if you feel comfortable to do so, otherwise droop your eyelids and bring your gaze to a spot or still object in front of you.

▶ Begin by noticing that you are breathing and notice the changes and sensations that come with the in breath and the out breath. Remain here, noticing these sensations for a few moments.

▶ Now gently slow down the rate of your breath. Breathe in for four to five seconds, pause and then breathe out for four to five seconds. Breathe in 1 – 2 – 3 – 4 – 5, pause for a moment, breathe out 1 – 2 – 3 – 4 – 5.

▶ If this feels too slow, begin at a rate that feels comfortable for you and take your time to slow the rate further.

▶ Bring your awareness to the sensations of your body and mind slowing down.

▶ Notice how your body responds to this slowing down.

▶ Continue to develop a rhythm that feels soothing for you for a few minutes.

▶ When you are ready, slowly open your eyes and notice a few objects in the room or space around you, to help ground you back into the environment that you are in.

How was that for you? If you found it difficult, that is OK, it can take time to get the hang of it and feel the calming effects. As mentioned, do use this exercise as much as you like, perhaps when you are feeling stressed, anxious and busier than ever. Taking a moment or two for self-care by soothing yourself in this way can work tremendously well, allowing you then to respond to your thoughts and feelings in a more helpful way. This will, then, allow you to choose and act on what matters most to you in that very moment.

Barriers to self-compassion

Before we come on to some more exercises, let us look at some common concerns that people often face when beginning to practise self-compassion.

'I don't deserve kindness'

For some of us, we may have learnt that being kind to ourselves is not safe or triggers difficult feelings, so our mind tries to protect us from this by suggesting that we stay well clear of it. If this sounds like you, it is possible that this is a message you received from an early age. Perhaps you did not receive a great deal of warmth and kindness from others so have learnt that, therefore, you are not worthy of any. It can take time to recognise your worth and, with practice, to realise that you and everyone around you deserves an abundance of kindness. Mindfulness can also help us to notice when we are avoiding being self-compassionate and habitually pulling back from it. Give it time and be gentle with you.

'I'll be letting myself off the hook and I won't get anything done!'

Many of us are so scared to let go of our critical mind, believing that, if we are instead kinder towards ourselves when we fail or make a mistake, we will become complacent, lazy and will get nothing done or, worse still, will not better ourselves in any way. We are wired to believe that self-criticism is the only means for self-improvement. Well, the research shows us that being kinder towards ourselves when we make a mistake is in, fact, a better motivator to then change our behaviour for the better. Think about it – when you are attacking yourself and feeling upset, low and/or anxious as a result, are you really in the best psychological state to think clearly and improve yourself or the situation you are in? Perhaps remind yourself of the 'Two teachers' exercise above to see what effect self-criticism, versus a kinder more compassionate self, has on you and your productivity to progress well in your life.

'My emotions are too powerful'

We know too well that, in the midst of an emotional storm, fight or flight mode really kicks in and the last thing on your mind is saying kind words to yourself or practising mindful breathing. However, the kindest and most useful act in that very moment might be simply to notice you are in a storm and reach a place of safety, then when it has died down a little, you can consider ways to be kind to yourself, as you are likely still to be hurting a great deal.

'Being kind to myself is a weakness/It's not a manly thing to do'

Compassion is about having the strength to face your fears, to bear witness to your pain so that you can choose a path that is best for you. Compassion is an act of courage. It is often confused with love, but the most important acts of compassion are towards aspects of our experience that we do not love, or even like. Consider your own experiences where you have faced a difficult challenge and, instead of finding a way out of it, stood up for something you believed in, despite your fear, or assertively expressed your needs, despite your anger towards another person; these all can be very difficult to do. Self-compassion is certainly not for the meek – it is about facing the reality of your pain head on and being bold enough to do something that may feel uncomfortable, all in the service of alleviating your undue suffering the best you can, and truly looking after yourself.

'I don't know how to'

Perhaps you have not had much experience of being kind to yourself. It is a concept many of us are not too familiar with. We are bombarded with messages like 'stiff upper lip', 'just get on with it', 'take your mind off things'. These are all too familiar for so many of us and can leave us a little deskilled in self-compassion. You may find it easier to consider how you treat others who you care about when they are struggling. Many of us find it much easier to show kindness to others and we can practise showing that same kindness to ourselves. Stay curious and see what shows up in your practices.

'It's selfish/self-indulgent, I should be thinking of others'

Self-indulgence is giving in to your feelings, perhaps skipping the gym after a hard day at work or eating lots of chocolate after an argument with a friend. Self-compassion is being wise to what is most helpful for your well-being in the long term, which often means the displeasure of heading to the gym. We also understand that it might seem that, if we pay attention to ourselves and our difficulties, it can be at a cost of paying attention to others and their needs. However, self-criticism and ignoring our own needs can leave us depleted and then we have little left to give. It is also worth considering that, if we treat ourselves kindly, then the people around us might be more encouraged to do the same for themselves. Consider the people you spend most time with – do they tend to treat themselves the same way you do? Self-compassion can be a little bit contagious!

If you are still sceptical about all this compassionate stuff, that is completely fine. We would still encourage you to have a go at the next two exercises, despite what your mind may be telling you. See if you can bring a genuine openness and curiosity to the experience of doing them, see what arises.

Practice 10.4: I haven't got time for this!

Loving you

▶ Close your eyes. Allow yourself to develop your soothing breathing rhythm.

▶ Take a few moments to imagine the face of someone you love with all your heart. Someone you care about very deeply.

▶ Imagine them looking in to your eyes. You begin to feel loved and safe.

▶ Allow the warmth connected to your loved one to wash over you. Take a few moments to savour that feeling.

▶ Now imagine your own face in front of you and that you, too, were someone you cared about deeply.

▶ What could you do today that told you 'I am loved'? How could you stop neglecting yourself and show yourself that you care about you?

▶ What one simple act could you do? It does not have to be grand, something small will do.

▶ Notice how it feels to reflect on looking after and loving yourself in this way.

Practice 10.5: Mindfulness right now!

Kind words

▶ Bring to mind something you are struggling with. Perhaps a conflict with a friend, a difficult decision, a stressful situation on the horizon, a recent mistake you made. Think about this difficulty for a few moments.

▶ See if you can really feel the emotions associated with this struggle and the discomfort in the body.

▶ Allow your breath to be an invitation to stillness. Engage in your soothing breathing rhythm, if that is helpful.

▶ Acknowledge that you are hurting, perhaps by saying to yourself, 'This is a moment of suffering' or 'This really hurts.'

▶ Let go of any judgements your mind makes about your pain, such as: 'There's something wrong with me,' 'I shouldn't feel like this,' 'I must be mad, I'm crazy, I'm weak and pathetic!'

▶ Place the palm of your hand gently over wherever in your body you feel the emotion most strongly.

▶ Remind yourself that suffering is part of life and that, although their circumstances may be different, others suffer just like you, too. You are not alone.

▶ Say to yourself kind words: 'I am human, no one is perfect,' 'I am here for you.'

▶ Ask yourself: what might be an expression of kindness to yourself? Perhaps saying, 'May I be kind to myself, may I be strong.'

▶ How else might you bring more compassion to your thinking and feelings?

Powerful imagery

Can you remember what you had for breakfast? Can you recall where you went on your last holiday and whether you enjoyed it? Do you remember who you spent your last birthday with? To be able to answer these questions, you are most likely using your skills in imagery.

We humans are pretty good at imagining things and, at times, it can be quite powerful, activating sensations in the body, emotions and further thoughts. For instance, try bringing to mind your favourite meal or snack. Really try to picture what it might look like and smell like. Stay with that for a moment and then imagine taking a bite into it. You might notice that, just by imagining your favourite meal, you have begun to slightly salivate or even feel hungry.

If you did not notice any changes in your body, how about you picture some food you really cannot stand the taste of or perhaps some food that is rotting and mouldy, with maggots crawling all over it. And then you take a big bite in to that . . . We are guessing that you are probably recoiling at the thought of that and feeling pretty grossed out. Sorry about that, it is just we really wanted to make an important point about how simply imagining things can create changes in our emotions, our bodies, our minds and, consequently, our actions in life.

Imagery can stimulate a range of physiological reactions and emotional experiences. Have a think about it. In the same way that you have a physiological response to thinking about food or perhaps sex, you would also have a physiological response to a fierce critical bully in your mind. If you beat yourself up all day long, it is likely that you would feel angry, depressed, anxious, tense and/or pretty wobbly most of the time. Similarly, therefore, if you had a kind, caring 'friend' in your mind, you would be more likely to feel calmer, safer and more soothed as you rush about your busy life. Our imagination is extremely powerful and the good news is that we can use it wisely if we choose to. We can apply this powerful tool to bringing compassionate changes to our thoughts, feelings and actions.

The fact is that the mind tends to be well rehearsed in imagining things that leave us feeling distressed and less skilled in imagining things that calm us. When flying, it is not uncommon for people to report imagining the plane falling from the sky, activating feelings of panic. Or, when a loved one does not arrive home when you expected them to, the mind is very skilled at imagining a whole host of potential worst-case scenarios, such as your loved one being run over by a bus, kidnapped or ending up in hospital, leaving us feeling very concerned indeed.

The good news is that we can strengthen our compassionate mind via imagining practices that are designed to cultivate feelings that help to soothe and calm us and the qualities that will help us to tolerate and cope with stress, suffering and all our busyness. Do not worry if you do not notice anything happening to begin with – it can take time and practice, just like all the exercises in this book. Have a go at practising this some more now.

Practice 10.6: I haven't got time for this!

Compassion for you

▶ Find a quiet space where you are unlikely to be disturbed.

▶ Begin slowly to engage in soothing rhythm breathing.

▶ If, at any point during the exercise, you find your mind wanders, simply allow space for this distraction and then, with the next out breath, bring your focus gently back.

▶ Bring your attention to your posture. Notice the strength in your body as it is grounded to the floor beneath it.

▶ Create a half smile to signify warmth and kindness.

▶ Begin to imagine a time when someone was very supportive of you. They were non-judgemental, they listened to you, cared about you and wanted to help you.

▶ Recall where you were at this time and what was happening around you. Look around your image and notice what you can see. Notice, too, what you can hear.

▶ See if you can really hear what this person said to you. Particularly notice the tone of their voice and the words they say to convey that they cared about you and understood what you were going through.

▶ Recall their body language and whether they did anything else to express compassion towards you.

▶ Acknowledge what emotions this person had for you. Notice how you feel in response to this. Acknowledge what it feels like in your own body for them to express these emotions towards you. See if you can create some space for these feelings, allowing feelings of compassion to flow in towards you.

▶ Stay with this image of receiving compassion and notice what feelings arise in your body.

▶ Connect with any feelings of gratitude or appreciation that may arise and stay present with these feelings, allowing them to linger for a few moments.

▶ When you are ready to do so, return your attention to your soothing rhythm breathing. Take a few moments to acknowledge that you have given yourself time to practise mindful self-compassion, to help alleviate your suffering in your busy life.

What did you notice during that exercise? It is possible that you may have noticed some of the feelings and qualities connected with self-compassion, such as warmth, closeness, kindness and care. If you did not, that is OK. Remember to take your time and give it another try when you can.

Walking the compassionate walk

We invite you to further your cultivation of self-compassion now by focusing on strengthening the specific qualities of your compassionate self.

Practice 10.7: Mindfulness right now!

Who is my compassionate self?

Take a few moments right now to perhaps jot down some of the qualities you would, ideally, like to have if you were someone who was truly calm, confident and compassionate towards yourself.

Here are a few ideas to start you off:

▶ The wisdom to know what is best for me.

▶ Empathy and understanding of my own suffering.

▶ Encouragement and kindness.

▶ Recognition that all humans suffer.

▶ Ability to face difficulty with strength.

Now spend a few moments to consider what a very compassionate person you might look like, sound like and behave like. How would they treat you when you are suffering?

OK, so, once you have some ideas jotted down, give the next practice a go.

Practice 10.8: I haven't got time for this!

You at your best

▶ Close your eyes and guide your attention towards your breathing. Engage with your soothing rhythm breathing.

▶ Remind yourself of the qualities of compassion that ideally you would have.

▶ Now imagine that you have all of these qualities. Breathe in wisdom, strength and kindness and breathe out, knowing that your mind is not your design. Breathe in understanding, non-judgement and empathy and breathe out knowing that your suffering is not your fault.

▶ Begin to imagine further what you might look like as a deeply compassionate person. Are you old or young? What are you wearing? What does your facial expression look like? How is your body posture, are you sitting or standing tall? Does your body language signal openness and care? Take a few moments to explore this image.

▶ Continue to follow your in breath and out breath as you imagine the qualities of compassion.

▶ Now, imagine what you might say to yourself when you are being someone who is caring, wise and strong. Notice the tone of your voice and whether you are loud or quiet.

▶ Imagine how you might be with yourself when you are suffering, what actions might you take? See if you can create space in your body for all the feelings that arise, welcoming them in to your experience right here, right now. Stay with this for a few moments.

▶ When you are ready to do so, return your awareness to your breathing. Remember that you can turn to this compassionate part of you at any moment in time. Take a moment right now to thank your mind for this experience. On the next exhalation, allow the images to fade away as you open your eyes and bring your attention to the space around you.

Engaging your compassionate self

As we invariably become caught up in our forever changing thoughts and feelings, it is as if we are alternating between different psychological states or parts of experiences. We have got an anxious self, an angry and critical self, an excited self and a compassionate self, and so on. When we are engaged with any of these experiences, they will have effects on our thoughts, feelings, bodily sensations, urges and behaviours. The interesting thing is that these different parts of our experience often interact with each other, so the angry part might communicate (or conflict) with the anxious part, and so on. This can be a difficult experience at times and often not the most helpful one to get caught up in as we try to manage the stresses and strains of our busy existence.

Sometimes, unearthing the compassionate part of ourselves is the best course of action we can take. Usually, it is the case that our anxious self and our angry self are, in fact, in desperate need of compassion, in order for us to get focused and productive, and moving towards what matters most to us once again. When activating our compassionate self, there is no need to challenge or suppress our anxious or angry inner voices; they tend to naturally settle and lower in volume, as they begin to feel looked after and soothed. Have a go at the next practice to experience the impact that your compassionate self can have on the other angry and anxious parts of you.

Practice 10.9: I haven't got time for this!

Taking a self-compassionate perspective

For this exercise, you might like to find a quiet room and arrange three separate chairs so that they are facing each other. You can then sit in each chair as you practise taking the perspective of different parts of your experience. Setting the chairs up in this way is not entirely necessary. However, you might like to try it to enhance your experience of the practice.

▶ Consider a difficult issue you have been facing recently. Notice how you have been responding to this issue. Perhaps the angry/self-critical and anxious/worried parts of you have shown up?

▶ Begin the practice first by taking on the role of the angry/self-critical you (perhaps sit in the first chair, designated to your angry/self-critical part). Express what thoughts and feelings you are having about this situation from that angry/self-critical perspective. Notice the words and tone of your voice. Notice your facial expression and body posture. How does this part of you want to handle the situation? Notice how you feel as you are taking on this role. Notice how your body feels as you become angry and berate yourself.

▶ Once you have done this, try taking on the role of your anxious/worried self (perhaps sit in the second chair, designated to the anxious/worried part of you) and repeat the step above. Noticing what it feels like to be talking from this anxious perspective about this difficult situation and where you feel that in your body.

▶ Now begin to notice how these two parts of you communicate, perhaps even arguing with each other. Continue to switch back and forth between each part of your experience (and seat) for a short while. Really try to experience how they feel and what it feels like to be on the receiving end of the other one.

▶ Now take a few moments to bring your attention to your breathing. Engage in your soothing rhythmic breathing.

▶ Now take a few moments to practise taking a more self-compassionate perspective (perhaps taking a seat in the third chair, designated to the self-compassionate part of your experience) and see if you can call upon your deepest care for yourself and your wisdom to address these other parts of you. What does your compassionate self want to say to the other parts of you to help them feel understood, cared for and listened to? Perhaps, this would be similar to what you might say to a distressed friend. Something like, 'I understand that you feel angry . . . I understand that you feel anxious . . . ' 'This is difficult for you right now, which makes sense, considering . . . '. 'I understand that by being self-critical/worrying you are trying to help, but it's not that helpful and there is an alternative . . . ' Allow your heart to open up and soften. What other words of compassion may be helpful? Perhaps, 'I am here with you both . . . it will be OK'

▶ What insights does this compassionate part of you have for your difficult situation? What wise advice would you give to yourself about how to best manage the situation, to best look after yourself? It is OK if you are not sure what to do or say; perhaps compassionately acknowledge that. Is there something kind you can do for yourself as you go through this? Remember to breathe, take time for yourself, look after yourself in some other way.

Remember that this compassionate part of you is always there, you can elicit it in any moment of time. Sometimes, it might just be a bit hidden away but, when we look for it, we can find it. Perhaps set an intention for yourself to approach this and other difficulties you encounter while being the compassionate you as much as possible. When we are at war with ourselves or attacking a particular part of ourselves, there can only ever be one loser! Consider, who would that be? Remember, mindful self-compassion is an effective alternative to this self-attacking stance that can help soothe all the other more painful parts of you, so that you can best navigate and manage your busy, stressful and demanding life.

Mindfulness top tips to-go

In this chapter, you have learned that it is helpful to do the following:

▶ Notice and let go of the high expectations that you place on yourself.

▶ Be kind to yourself when you are suffering, instead of criticising, berating and bullying yourself. This way, you will remain more behaviourally effective so you can do the things that matter most to you.

▶ Engage in your soothing rhythm breathing to help slow down the body and mind, helping you to regain control over your behaviour and your busy life.

▶ Practise self-compassion to increase your resilience in the face of stress and busyness.

CHAPTER

11

Mindful self-care

Well-being is fundamentally no different from learning to play the cello.

Richard Davidson – founder and chair of the Center for Healthy Minds

As we have seen from the previous chapter, we can cultivate a kinder, self-caring and more self-supporting way of being that offers us enormous benefits when navigating our way through our busy, hectic lives. In this chapter, we invite you to continue to increase your awareness of how you can better care for yourself with mindfulness, in the many different areas of your day-to-day life.

Body kindness

We all know that exercise and eating healthily are important for our physical health, but they can also be beneficial to our mental health and well-being, too. Both exercise and improving diet have been shown to reduce anxiety and depression and help people manage stressors more effectively.

Yet, our busy lives often can make it extremely difficult to find the time for daily exercise classes, going to the gym, sourcing healthy fresh ingredients and cooking from scratch. However, even very small changes to our daily routine can have a significant impact. Getting up from your desk every hour and moving your body for at least five minutes can burn 1,000 calories a week. Researchers have also found that 15 minutes of walking, five days a week, led to a 14 per cent lower risk of heart disease than those who did not do any exercise. That is just 1.5 per cent of a 16-hour day. The good news is that, by incorporating mindfulness into your walking each day, you are likely to experience even further benefits.

Most of us tend to walk around on autopilot while our minds usually are caught up in thoughts about all the things we need to do or places we need to get to. How often do you walk a familiar route (whether that be outdoors or from your bed to the bathroom or even across the office floor) only to arrive at your destination, realising you have noticed nothing along the way? How aware are you of your body and your surroundings when you walk? Have you ever really noticed the amazing intricacies and functionality of your body?

We just walk automatically, never really noticing or appreciating the splendid design and ability that our bodies have. The next exercise is all about bringing your awareness to the experience of walking, in the present moment. You can try this whenever you want, you just need to be walking. Try it as often as you can, even if it is only on a short walk from your bed to the bathroom first thing in the morning, across the office floor during the day or even to and from the canteen or train station each day.

Practice 11.1: I haven't got time for this!

Walkies

▶ As you begin to walk, first notice the sensations in your feet against the ground.

▶ Notice the automatic process and impulse of moving your legs. One leg rising and protruding forward to take the first step, then the next leg ready to follow with the second step.

▶ Notice the automatic impulses and movements in your arms.

▶ Notice what muscles tense or relax as you move your body to this thing we call walking.

▶ Acknowledge the weight of your body shifting between your left and right hip, your left and right leg, as you walk.

▶ Notice how you are stepping, the quality of each step (whether you are stepping hard or lightly onto the ground) the feel of your feet within your shoes and the ground beneath your feet.

▶ Become aware of the sensations of the air against your skin as you propel forwards. Notice the difference in sensations between areas that are exposed to the air and areas that are covered by clothes.

▶ How does the material of your clothing move against your skin as you walk?

▶ Expand your awareness to notice your surroundings.

▶ As you walk, what do you see, smell, hear, taste and feel?

▶ What do you notice around you? If this is a familiar walk, what do you notice that you never have before?

▶ Expand your awareness so that you remain aware of the sensations of walking and the external environment while you also become aware of your internal experiences, such as your thoughts and emotions.

▶ What thoughts cross your mind as you walk?

▶ What emotions are there right now? Are they intense or mild?

▶ Are these internal experiences pulling you in or can you observe them with a little bit of distance?

▶ No need to judge these internal experiences as good or bad, practise just noticing them for what they are.

▶ If, at any point during your walk, you notice your mind wandering to the past or the future or being pulled away from your experience of walking, just gently acknowledge that your mind has wandered and bring yourself back to the present moment and the experience of walking.

▶ Remember that being pulled away and coming back is the key to mindfulness practice.

You can also move your body with mindfulness in ways other than walking. Bringing mindfulness to running, other types of sport or exercise, stretching or just some simple body movements can be re-energising, assist with maintaining your fitness and help you to cultivate your practice of present moment awareness. Try out the next practice as an alternative to mindful walking.

Practice 11.2: I haven't got time for this!

Mindful movement

▶ Lie down on your back with your legs stretched out and arms by your side, palms towards the ground.

▶ As you inhale, slowly raise your arms behind your head and stretch them towards the ground. Notice any sensations in your ribs, shoulders and arms.

▶ As you exhale, return your arms to your sides and notice the changes in sensations in your body. Repeat for three to five breaths.

▶ Now, on the next inhalation, bring one of your knees slowly to your chest and squeeze with your arms. Notice the sense of tension.

▶ As you exhale, lower your leg once again. Then switch legs. Repeat for three to five breaths.

▶ Now, as you inhale, bring both of your knees to your chest and pull them in with your arms. Lower them gently as you exhale. Repeat for three to five breaths.

▶ Roll over to the side and gently bring yourself to a standing position, pausing here for a few breaths. Notice the blood flowing through your body as you make this movement.

▶ On your next inhalation, reach your right arm over your head as you bend to the left and, at the same time, lower your left arm down your body. Exhale, return to centre. Repeat on the other side. Repeat for three to five breaths.

▶ Standing tall, on the next in breath, sweep both arms outwards and raise them above your head. Reach up high and feel the stretch throughout your arms and torso. On the exhalation, lower your arms to your side. Repeat for three to five breaths.

Healthy eating

Just as we can become easily distracted in thought whilst walking and moving around, so too can we become distracted when we eat. We can end up scoffing a whole family-sized bag of crisps, when we were intending to have only a handful. For many, the busy mind can result in eating when we are no longer hungry, as our attention is taken away from internal cues telling us we are full.

Eating well can help to prevent all sorts of diseases and improve our mental health. Studies have shown that the risk of depression increases by around 80 per cent when comparing teenagers who have a low-quality diet compared to those eating a higher-quality diet. Nourishing food quite literally nourishes the mind and a healthy gut improves mood and cognition.

Further, practising mindful eating can help us to make healthier food choices. Try out the following practice using a small piece of food, such as an orange segment, a nut or biscuit. Remember, you do not need to think about the piece of food to really experience it, use your senses to truly savour what you eat. Give it a try right now.

Practice 11.3: I haven't got time for this!

Mindful meal-time

▶ Place your piece of food in the palm of your hand. Notice the weight and how much space it takes up in your palm.

▶ Take a moment to really see your piece of food in front of you. Explore the colours and textures, moving the piece of food around so you can see any variations.

▶ Close your eyes and notice what it feels like. Is it firm or squidgy, moist or dry?

▶ Bring it close to your nose and see if you can notice any particular smell. If there is no smell, notice what that is like and acknowledge the absence of smell.

▶ Place the food gently between your lips and notice any sensations here.

▶ Now, without biting, move it on to your tongue and hold it here for a few moments. Notice any changes occurring in your mouth and notice if you can experience any taste.

▶ Slowly bite in to your food and really notice the movement of your mouth and jaw and the sensation of chewing. Notice if the taste changes as you continue chewing.

▶ Notice the sensation of the food item moving to the back of your throat before swallowing. Follow any sensations down in to your stomach.

▶ Once you have finished eating, notice the sensation of an absence of food in your mouth.

▶ Take a moment to acknowledge how your body is now one piece of food heavier.

It can be helpful to do this practice very slowly to begin with, but it is not necessary to eat slowly in order to eat mindfully. Perhaps, when you feel ready to do so, try to eat a meal mindfully, without changing the speed you would eat at normally. Mindfulness in this way, and in many of the other practices throughout the book, not only helps us to notice our internal body cues to feelings of fullness and hunger, but also helps people to resist cravings.

Here are a few other ideas for switching up your routine that take little time out of your day and that demonstrate kindness to the needs of your body.

▶ Take the stairs instead of using the lift.

▶ Walk to the next bus stop.

▶ Park in the furthest car park space.

▶ Take a stretch or do some gentle yoga when you wake up.

▶ Get up and move about after every 20 minutes of sitting still.

▶ Try jogging on the spot during TV ads.

▶ Play outdoors with your children.

▶ Do something different with your body while watching TV – sit on the floor, walk around while you are on the phone.

▶ Learn a new recipe, incorporating healthier ingredients.

▶ Swap fizzy drinks for water flavoured with cucumber or lemon slices.

▶ Choose foods with the least number of ingredients.

▶ Notice the smell, colour and textures of your food before eating.

Sleepiness

Sleep is needed to save energy and organise the mind, laying down networks for memory and learning. Theory suggests that the energy we save during sleep is used for brain functions, immune functions and tissue growth. If we do not get enough sleep, our functioning in all areas deteriorates and we become vulnerable to infections. Poor sleepers are also more likely to be: obese and inactive, at increased risk for cancer and cardiovascular disease, low in mood, more dissatisfied in their relationships and performing less well on tasks involving memory, concentration and decision making.

This is not ideal for times when our busy life requires us to be on top form, so it is important that we give some mindful attention to sleep.

Normally, if you feel tired, our highly psychologically insightful recommendation would be . . . to sleep. This is sometimes easier said than done when you are really busy and your mind is racing and you are, basically, a tad frenetic. Nevertheless, if you are even able to notice, then the good news is, you are at least aware of your need for more rest. And the even better news is that we can get a lot of rest just by resting in awareness (even more than when running from the boogieman when we are fast asleep). Try this next mindfulness exercise as soon as you can. Here are some helpful pointers:

▶ For the purposes of this practice, it makes no difference if you fall asleep or not.

▶ If you do have to be somewhere, it might be useful to decide how long you want to practise before beginning and set an alarm or have someone gently wake you, if you do fall asleep.

▶ Simply practise awareness of whatever experiences arise, thoughts, feelings, sensations, urges, sleepiness and sleeplessness, just notice these come and go.

▶ It may be that as you practise this you become aware of how punitive you are usually to pushing away your tiredness and refusing to sleep – a basic physical need. Or how your eagerness and anxiety to fall asleep causes more restlessness and gets in the way of any restfulness and potential sleep.

Practice 11.4: I haven't got time for this!

Duvet-diving mindfulness

This takes about 60 seconds – or all day, if you want:

▶ Get yourself comfy and allow yourself to settle into this moment, in your bed.

▶ Notice the position of your body, just as it is.

▶ Become aware of the contact of the duvet with your body.

▶ Become aware of the sensations where your body makes contact with the soft bouncy mattress.

▶ Observe any warmth, softness and cosiness around you.

▶ Observe any restlessness or fidgeting in your body.

▶ Keep returning to these sensations of warmth, softness, cosiness, developing an interest and curiosity in them.

▶ Be aware of thoughts arising, perhaps urges to fall asleep or get up, try staying just as you are and watch those thoughts and urges drifting around.

▶ Bring your focus of attention to now, the sensations, softly held in your duvet.

▶ There you are, in your bed, aware of postures, all sensations, emotions, thoughts.

▶ Just for this moment, there is nothing else to do.

Here are our top tips for sleep:

▶ Increase your opportunity for sleep by getting a regular routine of seven to eight hours of resting and sleeping in bed.

▶ If you are lying awake in bed, practise mindfulness and let go of trying to get to sleep. Simply resting is much better than fighting to try to get to sleep and you may also find that you drift off naturally without trying.

▶ Wind down at least 45 minutes before bed by dimming the lights, doing something relaxing that does not require thinking and getting ready for bed.

▶ Stop drinking caffeine after midday. Caffeine is a stimulant and takes four hours for just half the amount of caffeine to leave the body.

▶ Finish eating any heavy meal or doing any exercise at least two hours before you go to bed. Avoid drinking alcohol before going to bed.

Physical discomfort

Being busy most of the time leads to high levels of adrenaline rushing around our bodies. This is just the case, even if we are busy in our minds and not that physically active from day to day. Our bodies can tell us quite a lot about how busy and stressed we are in any given moment. For many of us busy people, it is not until we notice our heart beating fast, a shortness of breath, a headache, feeling dizzy, shaky, lethargic or that we pull a muscle or whack our toe on the edge of a door – or a combination of the above – that we even realise that we have been rushing around on autopilot, stressed out, for far too long.

Everyone who sits still for a period of time (with your nose pressed up against a computer screen at your desk) inevitably will experience a level of discomfort, especially if you are not used to it.

When we make adjustments mindfully, and come to a place of rest and stillness, then we see the merit in movement and we are acting towards self-care. Awareness of this can be very beneficial. Lack of awareness can leave us living with discomfort we might not be responding to in the most effective way; we can be prone to ignoring our discomfort, disowning it, being frustrated, dismissive and irritated with it. The pain in my a*se is so annoying, it is a real pain in the a*se and so are you! And the world around you!

These responses to physical representations of discomfort are absolutely the same as we have towards mental and emotional discomfort. Awareness and acceptance can lead to acknowledgements and the need for change as an expression of self-care (just like getting an extra cushion for our a*se to sit on, drinking when thirsty or, perhaps, a realisation that you need to resolve a disagreement with someone). Alternatively, awareness of habitual tendencies of fidgeting, ignoring the problem and/or 'getting on with it' may be noticed as unhelpful.

Short-term pain or discomfort

Short-term pain, discomfort or even illness, although unpleasant, often are tolerated, but have a sense of transience so, unless recurrent, are not as distressing as long-term illness because usually we relate to them differently. We can be dismissive and stoic, 'carrying on', especially when we have so much to get done, knowing we will probably get over it soon (although this can be very damaging if we do this too much). We can use over-the-counter medications, do some simple stretching or use other ways to take care of ourselves and, sometimes, this is sufficient to 'make it go away'.

The desire to take away pain is a natural and quite instinctive approach, but often we do not even notice that we are doing it. Our bodies have a helpful way of continuing to niggle at discomfort that needs more attention, even when we might be ignoring it. A very itchy mosquito bite, calling to you to please, please give it a scratch, for example, or an injury reminding you not to put too much weight on that part of your body, or perhaps a persistent cough.

With even the most paltry amount of mindfulness, usually we learn what to do pretty quickly, often quite reactively – 'surf' the urge to scratch, keep weight off an injury, get out of the cloud of toxic smoke. However, what if the discomfort keeps on going, the bite does not stop itching, the injury does not heal, the cough comes back? Then we can find ourselves beginning to build stories to go with the discomfort: the bite becomes a tropical disease, the injury a permanent disability, the cough cancer – oh my, I will never be able get everything done in time now and will just get busier and busier.

These stories may or may not be true. Usually, they are catastrophic, dramatic and unbearable and we, again, instinctively want to get away from them and our pain as quickly as possible. We create suffering through our habitual responses to pain or discomfort, when we have pain *and* suffering, life can feel really appalling.

This can even become cyclical: pain arises, we push it away, it arises again, we tell ourselves a 'danger story'; now we experience mental suffering and physical pain, we push it away, pain arises, the story-telling becomes more embellished, we suffer more, we attach to our stories emotionally and they feel true, this is verified to us through the experience of physical pain, the pain becomes more threatening, our body becomes more tense, further pain arises, etc. In fact, it is entirely possible to have physical pain that is totally stress-related.

Guess what? Mindfulness simply requires attention to the pain and discomfort, to attend to our habitual way of responding. No need to push it away, no need to attach to our stories, just to notice. The pain may or may not disappear, but our suffering can. When we are clear from suffering, we may also find ourselves able to relate differently to our pain once we have noticed just exactly what we are dealing with.

Long-term pain or illness

The biggy here, of course, is long-term health-related issues, which can feel unbearable. But this, too, can be assisted with mindfulness. Unlike our (sometimes) helpful aversion to minor discomfort or pain, which can involve a simple act such as taking medicine or shifting position to functionally aid our bodies, long-term or chronic pain is made extremely difficult to live with when we are so averse to it.

Ignoring, distracting or temporarily suppressing pain or discomfort, when it is chronic, does not work. With chronic pain, the key is to accept and then to explore and investigate our relationship, to be open to our natural attachment to suffering and to cultivate compassion (see more on this in Chapter 10). Mindfulness is not about accepting pain in order to endure, suffer and be wilful. With mindfulness, such as with the following body exercise, you learn about how you are relating to your pain, you can find openness to now, to be in just one moment at a time, to learn ways to live, just as you are.

Practice 11.5: I haven't got time for this!

Body watching

This is a quick exercise to help you to begin to develop a more helpful relationship with your body and any experiences of discomfort and pain. Wherever you are, whatever you are engaged with – be it on the train, preparing a report for work, getting the children ready for a bath, writing an email or checking your mobile phone – take three minutes to tune into your body.

- ▶ Tune into any bodily sensations that you can notice as you continue with your task.
- ▶ Acknowledge and label them like a curious scientist might – 'There is a tightness in my chest' or 'There is an ache in my head.'
- ▶ If your mind comes in to judge this, try to acknowledge your thoughts and return to just noticing and observing the sensation.
- ▶ Finally, notice your posture and stance, scanning your body from head to toe, observing the body in its entirety, whatever you may be doing.

This practice can be done at any time during any activity you may be doing. If you like, you could take some more time to try out the next body scan practice. This will help you further to cultivate present moment awareness in relation to your body and the forever changing sensations that pass through it. Practising this exercise regularly will strengthen your ability to open up to painful sensations in your body, rather than persisting to struggle with them, which, invariably, will lead only to more suffering on top of any bodily pain you might experience.

Practice 11.6: I haven't got time for this!

Body scanning

The purpose of this practice is to cultivate a non-judging awareness of your body, moment by moment. Allowing any thoughts, feelings and urges simply to come and go, rise and fall, as you remain aware of your body throughout.

▶ Sit or lay somewhere comfortably. Close your eyes or droop your eyelids and let your gaze rest on a still object or spot in front of you.

▶ Begin by bringing your awareness to your feet. Allow your feet to take centre stage in your awareness right now.

▶ You may notice a sensation at your feet, perhaps the sensation of your feet against the floor or touching the inside of your shoes. You may notice an absence of sensation at your feet. Either is fine, the presence or absence of sensation. Remember, this exercise is not about sensation but about awareness of what is, just as it is.

▶ As you notice your feet in this way, your mind may give you some thoughts, such as judgements, opinions and preferences, about the practice itself or about anything else at all. These thoughts may distract you and pull your attention away.

▶ Simply notice the distraction, perhaps label the distraction thinking, congratulate yourself for noticing this and then gently guide your attention back into your feet.

▶ There they are again, the left and right foot, and then there is you, noticing your feet in this moment.

▶ Next, allow your feet to dissolve from your awareness and bring your awareness to your legs.

▶ Acknowledge the position of your legs as you sit or lie as you are.

▶ Notice the sensations or absence of sensations at your legs.

▶ There they are, your legs, and then there is you, holding them at centre stage in your awareness. Just these legs, just this moment.

▶ Next, allow your legs to dissolve from your awareness and then bring your awareness to your arms.

▶ Again, notice the position of your arms, just as they are right now. Notice any changing sensations or absence of sensations in your arms.

▶ Next, be as curious and open as you can to notice the sensation of air where it meets the surface of your skin. You may notice the sensation of air against your skin on your face, neck, hands or any exposed or other body part. Stay with this for a few minutes and see what arises.

▶ Next, begin to scan your body from the tip of your head to the tips of your toes. Scan up and down and acknowledge any warmer sensations you come across versus cooler ones. It may be warmer where your body makes contact with the surface that you are sitting or lying on. Or it may be warmer where different body parts are resting against one another. Acknowledging these warmer sensations is much like tipping your hat or nodding your head to a passer-by on the street to acknowledge them – 'Ah! Warmer sensation, I see you!' Keep scanning for these warmer sensations for a minute or two.

▶ Notice where your attention is now. If it is not scanning your body for warmer sensations, then gently bring it back to doing just that.

▶ When you are ready, bring your awareness to your feet once again, as you did at the start. Maybe marvelling at the amazing ability you have to expand or narrow your awareness at your will.

▶ So, there they are again, your two feet. With the presence or absence of sensation. Then there is you, observing your feet, in this very moment. Just these two feet, just this one moment.

▶ When you are ready, bring to mind some of the objects that are around you and gently begin to open your eyes, grounding yourself back into the environment, bringing the same present moment awareness with you as you go about your day.

People often report how they feel relaxed, calm or tranquil after doing an exercise like this. How was it for you? If you did feel relaxed, it is important to remember that you did not do a relaxation exercise but an exercise of the mind, called resting in awareness and, in this case, of your body. If you did feel this way, it is likely that you were less caught up in any thoughts or other distractions and, instead, more present to your unfolding experience moment by moment, using your body as an anchor to the here and now.

Bringing mindfulness to our body in practices like these helps us to recognise how we are more expansive and greater than the forever changing experiences of our body, including sensations and emotions and thoughts in our minds. The truth is that your body does change, it is always changing. It is not the same body you had as a young child. You may have had things cut out or put into your body. The skin on the surface of your body changes. You may have grown hair in places and lost hair in others. The temperature of your body can change day to day, moment to moment. It can feel hot, it can feel cold. Your body can feel tired and lethargic and it can feel energised at other times. Your body can hurt and feel painful, it can feel weak and, at other times, it can feel strong and relaxed.

The experiences and sensations of your body change, just like the ever-changing thoughts in your mind and emotions passing through you, but the *you* that notices and is aware of all these changing experiences never changes. That remains stable, unchanged and constant.

Self-appreciation

Chances are that you are reading this, wearing something. You may, even, have washed, eaten, had something to drink, taken any medication you might need, exercised and had some sleep (not necessarily in that order). If you have done any, all or more of these kinds of things, you have engaged in acts of self-care. Perhaps you did not notice this or are, even now, dismissing this with a 'Pish! Why, of course!' We hope so, because then you are also able to recognise quickly how easily you disregard these everyday activities, how habituated you are to not noticing your frequent gestures of care towards yourself and you know well enough by now that this mindfulness stuff is about noticing all of that and probably more.

When we adopt an attitude of ease, perhaps reminding ourselves of this when we find ourselves too caught up in rushing for impossible deadlines, killing ourselves over the latest diet fad or straining to fit in one more rep at the gym, just maybe we can take a step back – seeing everything we are up to as it is, realising it can be quite simple just to let go and exhale into the next moment.

We can even appreciate the misguided assumptions of our mind – which are so busy struggling to 'get it right', 'be better' or 'be perfect' – and remind ourselves that this tactic has not been working so well; in fact, for all that effort, it is pretty much a dud deal. Why not try congratulating yourself for trying something different, for all the mindfulness practices you have participated in, for all the ways you have already helped create new neural pathways to genuine well-being and success instead?

Self-appreciation sometimes can feel a bit uncomfortable if we have been led to believe that blowing our own trumpet is somehow vain, embarrassing or conceited. It is helpful to remind yourself that self-appreciation is not about being superior or striving for perfection, it is about noticing and allowing yourself to be free from these things and to fully experience life, and that includes you!

To add to this, do you realise that, according to physicists, we are made of the same basic atomic components as the stars? American astrologer, Carl Sagan wrote:

> The nitrogen in our DNA, the calcium in our teeth, the iron in our blood, the carbon in our apple pies were made in the interiors of collapsing stars. We are made of starstuff.

We think that that is definitely something to appreciate about ourselves and also to recognise that, without the particles that made us, the apple pie or the universe and all its infinite mysteries, would not be complete. Not only are you matter, you *really matter*.

Practice 11.7: I haven't got time for this!

Mirror, mirror on the wall . . .

▶ Whenever you next find yourself near a mirror, preferably in private, stop and take a good look at yourself.

▶ Look deep into your own eyes and notice how they shine like the stars (because they really do).

▶ Remember to breathe.

▶ Notice what thoughts may arise, perhaps judgement, criticisms or appraisals.

▶ See if you can let go of the content of these thoughts and, gazing deeply at yourself, marvel at your amazing capacity to have thoughts and intelligence.

▶ Looking into your eyes, breathing, take a moment to wonder at your body's wisdom in allowing you to see, to breathe and to be as well as you are (however well that may be), sustaining your life.

▶ Take this moment to appreciate yourself in whatever ways you wish. You might even like to try a sneaky smile and see that miraculous person just in front of you smiling right back at you.

Social connection

Other people or circumstances often can appear to be the very cause of our problems so we can be inclined to keep away or emotionally cut ourselves off. We elbow the charity hawker out of the way, scream cathartically at the telesales person or ignore phone calls and withdraw from loved ones, as we are desperately attempting to defend and preserve our tiny patch of space to breathe.

This route can become one of intense isolation, loneliness and despair. We hope you have seen that there is a way back. In fact, the way back is here, now and in this very moment. The second you wake up to this, you open to self-compassion and there you have the antidote. Quite simply, forget about the other people who need your help, want your money, time or that very breath. It might *look* nice and sweet to give them your time, money or breath as you are screaming on the inside, but our guess is that someone else might be needing some good attention right now. We increase the universal suffering quota only if we do not start by giving some care and acceptance to ourselves first. It is simply unhelpful to give any of our time, money, breath, kindness, or anything, to anything or anyone else if we have not even got enough ourselves.

We can also recognise the way that others might play on this by taking advantage of our busyness, gullibility, guilt and our desire to make the world better, when we respect our sense of self-compassion and care. Others taking time, money, energy that we do not have is simply unkind to us, but equally by giving that which we do not have, we can be unkind to ourselves, too.

Genuine acts of compassion and care are heartfelt – not derived from our autopilot reactions, aversion to difficult emotions or grasping at the 'feel-good factor'. Self-compassion, as outlined in the previous chapter, recharges our 'compassion fatigue', so we can then become re-energised and re-engaged with the suffering of those around us in an authentic way. In other words, we need to put our oxygen masks on first and breathe deeply before we can help those around us.

A further aspect of self-care is, therefore, how it serves to increase our sense of connection to others. We are all aware of the irony that in our modern-day lives, with the amount of social media that we have at our fingertips and our ability to travel to the far corners of the globe, the rates of relationship break-downs and sense of isolation and loneliness are higher than ever. Long lists of friends do not necessarily equate to a sense of belonging or closeness.

> A human being is a part of a whole, called by us 'universe', a part limited in time and space. He experiences himself, his thoughts and feelings as something separated from the rest . . . a kind of optical delusion of his consciousness. This delusion is a kind of prison for us, restricting us to our personal desires and to affection for a few persons nearest to us. Our task must be to free ourselves from this prison by widening our circle of compassion to embrace all living creatures and the whole of nature in its beauty.
>
> **Albert Einstein**

Again, the great news is that we have a *lot* of universe around us. Your particular patch may be very full of life indeed. This little microcosm you call 'work', 'home', 'park' or 'planet earth' is probably teeming with it. All this life busy bustling along on your keyboard, phone, street or in the skies. Every weeny bacteria or bull elephant bumbling about somewhere upon this floating ball in space, probably getting lost in their own navels, too. We are surrounded. Life is right here in our faces and making a right old racket about it.

We have an abundance of micro-moments that can lead to connection with others, yet often we miss out on these opportunities. We miss out on seeing our loved one's strengths, beauty, joys and triumphs, our friend's suffering or how strangers share in our humanity and the complexities of life. We miss out on these opportunities as we are usually too busy; busy running from the part of ourselves that we do not like. Rather than looking after ourselves and meeting our experience with acceptance, we are rejecting ourselves, which is such a distracting affair – to truly love others we must first be truly willing to love ourselves.

Some of our relationships, particularly those with our nearest and dearest, can, of course, be extremely challenging at times. Other people can do and say things to us that bring up our deepest insecurities and vulnerability. We can charge forth, defensively in response to this pain with anger and frustration and it is in this protective state that it can be very difficult to feel compassion towards others. Taking care of ourselves first and meeting our experience with acceptance and kindness is crucial in helping us to stay connected to others.

Try the following practice when you are next in the midst of a challenging situation or conflict with anyone – your partner, your friend, your boss, the shop assistant.

Practice 11.8: I haven't got time for this!

Managing conflict

▶ In the midst of the conflict, notice that you are breathing. Notice the quality of your breath. Follow your breath a few times. Notice any sensations around your heart – is it beating fast, slow?

▶ Notice how you are feeling. Anger, resentment, disappointment? What lies beneath this feeling? Invalidation, rejection, vulnerability?

▶ Accept this feeling with care and kindness. You do not have to like it, just be willing to have it.

▶ What is this feeling telling you that you want and need? Perhaps you want to be treated differently, be understood, be respected, accepted, loved?

▶ Bring your attention to what the other person needs, perhaps asking them, if necessary. See if you can acknowledge your pain and the pain of the other person. This person, just like you, can feel sad, angry and hurt at times.

▶ Notice any thoughts arising. Let go of any judgements that your mind may be producing, perhaps about how you and the other person feels. How you or the other person should feel and behave.

▶ Listen to the other person. Bring your full awareness to what is happening right now. There is nothing else but this.

▶ Once the conversation has ended, acknowledge how you are feeling. Accept this feeling with care and kindness. You do not have to like it, just be willing to have it.

▶ Bring your attention to what you appreciate in the other person and yourself.

▶ Congratulate yourself for being fully present with this other human being.

▶ Perhaps, even if you still feel angry, you could repeat these few words silently if you wish with the other person in mind, 'may you be well, may you find release, may you be happy'.

Tracking your practice

In Part 4, we have explored ways that you can take better care of yourself in different contexts of your busy life. We suspect that some of these exercises might feel a little unusual to begin with. Do make a note of whatever your experience has been. We also recommend that you highlight any favourite ones that you can come back to and practise again.

Practice	Page	When?	Notes
10.3: Soothing rhythm breathing	144	Practise it as often as possible. We would recommend at least once a day for several minutes and especially when you are feeling distressed.	
10.5: Kind words	148	Practise this whenever you notice yourself struggling.	
10.8: You at your best	153	At any moment in time when you are struggling and in need of some support.	
11.1: Walkies	159	Whenever you are walking. Try it once or twice over the next week.	
11.2: Mindful movement	160	As often as you want perhaps in the morning as part of your morning routine.	
11.3: Mindful meal-time	161	Whenever you are eating. Try it once or twice over the next week.	
11.4: Duvet-diving mindfulness	164	Any time you are struggling to sleep or may want to get some rest in bed.	

Practice	Page	When?	Notes
11.5: Body watching	168	Throughout the day, while you are doing any activity.	
11.6: Body scanning	169	Whenever you want, maybe when you are lying in bed at night or when you wake up in the morning, perhaps once or twice a week.	
11.7: Mirror, mirror on the wall . . .	172	Next time you look in the mirror.	
11.8: Managing conflict	175	When there is a conflict in any relationship (at work, with family, with friends, with a waiter – anyone!).	

Part

5

Mindfulness and moving forward

In this last part of the book we are going to:

▶ Help you to figure out what matters the most to you; you – values.

▶ Show you how mindfulness can help move you towards your values.

▶ Remind you how your awareness is abundant, with you always in every moment.

▶ Show you how you will know that mindfulness is working for you.

▶ Provide you with tips for when it feels like mindfulness is not working or is too difficult to do.

▶ Highlight why mindfulness is so popular and why it is important to us all in this modern world.

▶ Give you some suggestions for further reading, useful contacts and resources.

12

Living a meaningful life

Where am I going?

When our busy lives throw up so many challenges and problems to solve, we can be thrown off course and lose sight of where we are heading. We can be pulled in to the rat race easily without ever realising how we even got there. When we are on autopilot mode, it can be helpful to put on the brakes now and again and check we are on the right path. So far throughout the book we have explored ways to practise putting on the brakes, through noticing our experiences as they are. In this chapter, we want to turn your attention to reconnecting with your preferred direction in life, the one that is truly where you want to head. This chosen direction is based on what you care about, what is important to you and what gives you the most meaning in your life; your values.

Research shows us that having a clear sense of direction, or meaning and purpose in life, not only improves our well-being, but also helps us to live longer, cope better with the inevitable challenges throughout our busy existence and reduce cognitive decline as we age. So, perhaps it is time to start thinking about what truly matters the most to you, and ensure that you are moving in that direction.

Our inner compass

As a child, you may have been asked, 'Who do you want to *be* when you grow older?' But, now, instead, we tend to get asked, 'What do you *do* for work?', 'What do you do in your spare time?'. As we grow up, we can forget easily about our internal, personal values, our aspirations of the type of person we want to be, the type of life we want to be living and, instead, end up focusing on what we are doing, what we can achieve and all the goals we want to meet, which often are based on what we think we 'should' be doing and how we 'should' be as a person.

Our choices, behaviours and actions are, therefore, usually based on all these 'shoulds' produced by our minds, rather than on what we truly hold dear in our hearts. Society often encourages us to be goal-oriented, to get things done so that we can feel good. Pass your exams, get a job, get married, have babies, get a promotion, buy a house, and so on. Goals are not a problem per se, it is just that, if those goals are disconnected from our values, it can lead to an unfulfilling and miserable life.

The fisherman and the businessman

A fisherman was lying on a beautiful beach, enjoying the warmth of the sun after catching several big fish. A businessman came walking down the beach to relieve some of the stress of his workday and decided to find out why this fisherman had stopped fishing. 'Why don't you stay in the sea and catch more fish?' asked the businessman.

'This is enough to feed my whole family,' the fisherman said.

The businessman then asked, 'So, how do you spend the rest of your day?'

The fisherman replied, 'Well, I usually wake up early in the morning, go out to sea and catch a few fish, then go back and play with my kids. In the afternoon, I take a nap with my wife and, when evening comes, I join my buddies in the village for a drink — we play the guitar, sing and dance throughout the night.'

The businessman offered a suggestion to the fisherman:

'I have a PhD in business management. I could help you to become a more successful fisherman. From now on, you should spend more time at sea and try to

➤

catch as many fish as possible. When you have saved enough money, you could buy a bigger boat and catch even more fish. Soon you will be able to afford to buy more boats, set up your own company, your own production plant for canned food and a distribution network. By then, you will have moved out of this village and to Sao Paulo, where you can set up HQ to manage your other branches.'

The fisherman continues, 'And after that?'

The businessman laughs heartily, 'After that, you can live like a king in your own house and, when the time is right, you can go public and float your shares in the Stock Exchange, and you will be rich.'

The fisherman asks, 'And after that?'

The businessman says, 'After that, you can finally retire, you can move to a house by the fishing village, wake up early in the morning, catch a few fish, then return home to play with kids, have a nice afternoon nap with your wife and, when evening comes, you can join your buddies for a drink, play the guitar, sing and dance throughout the night! You won't have a care in the world!'

The fisherman, smiling, looked up and said, 'Isn't that what I am doing right now?'

Connecting with our deeply held, personal values, on the other hand, can help direct us towards a life that is really alive, full of vitality and what really counts. We can think of our values as an inner compass to reorient ourselves to a direction that matters the most to us, a life worth living – one chosen by you. The following analogy helps to remind us that the opportunity for contentment and well-being has been right in front of us (or within us) all along, in the gift of our values.

We are not suggesting that we spend all day on the beach, dancing and having fun, although that does sound appealing to us. But, ask yourself honestly whether, like the businessman in the story above, you too comfort yourself with the thought that, once all the items on the to-do list are 'done and dusted', once you have achieved all that you want to in life, then you will get to live the life you want. The problem with this approach is that many of the concrete things that you might want to accomplish could be out of your control, to a certain degree or for some time anyway, leading to you feeling dissatisfied and that your life is lacking in some way. Now, consider how, perhaps, just maybe you can start living the life you want right now, even with all the busyness and despite what you may not have achieved. What if living a satisfying and meaningful life was actually already in your control and more about how you chose to be, day to day?

You may be very familiar with *to-do lists*. You might have them dotted all over your desk, at home, stuck on the fridge or have fancy colour coordinated spreadsheets on your computer. The mind is very good at churning these out, but have you ever thought of creating a *to-be list*? This can be a helpful way to reorient us to tasks that actually matter. Try out the following practice and see if it can become a new way to start your day.

Practice 12.1: Mindfulness right now!

To-be list

▶ What kind of person do I want to *be* today (e.g. kind, caring, supportive, hardworking, fun)?

▶ What aspects of my life do I wish to *be* paying more attention to (e.g. health, relationships, personal development, fitness, work)?

▶ When I look back on my day, how do I hope to have *been* with myself (e.g. kind, compassionate)?

▶ What is the most important thing I want to *be* in my life?

▶ How would I like to *be* at work today?

▶ How do I want to *be* when confronted with the challenges of the day?

Your values are all yours

Rather than rigid goals, values can be described as our personally desired and freely chosen life directions, driven by what is most important to us, deep in our hearts. They are what contributes to your life being full, rich, meaningful and rewarding and, in other words, what truly matters to you. More specifically, rather than something or a goal that we attain (which, ultimately, may be out of our reach or control), values describe the qualities that we would prefer to bring to our actions and live by in life and within the different roles we have (for example, how you wish to be as a partner, friend, colleague). The qualities that we bring to our actions are very much within our control. In other words, our values are how we choose to behave and what we want to stand for in any given situation.

What matters most to you, deep down in your heart, is entirely down to you and the experiences you have had in your life. No one else gets a say on what values you should or should not consider important. Yet, so often, our actions can be guided by our family's values, what our friends think, advertisements in magazines and on TV and what society tells us. Your values are not dependent on others' opinions and they will continue to exist whether or not others witness you living by them. The other reason that so many of us do not choose to live by our own personal values is that it isn't always easy to do and can be uncomfortable. For example, working hard might mean doing tasks that you find dull or boring; being affectionate and loving in a relationship might leave you feeling vulnerable and open to rejection; learning new skills might lead you to feel incompetent and remind you of how much you still don't know etc. However, it is important to remember that by taking more value-driven actions your life becomes more fulfilling and meaningful.

With the next exercises, we invite you to explore your own personal values. It can help to describe them as if no one will ever find out about them. You do not have to think or feel your values, you just choose them. The other important thing to remember is that they are not fixed either. What becomes more or less important to you can change in any moment and in any context or in the many different roles that you may fulfil in life. For example, you may value being romantic in your relationship, but this may not be a value you wish to live by in your work. Also, although you may value being romantic in your relationship, you may also value being honest with your partner, which may not seem romantic at times.

Sometimes, your values can seem conflicting in this respect and when that happens it can be useful to ask yourself the question: *which is most important to me right now, in this moment, and in this context?* It is, therefore, important to hold your values loosely and it can be helpful to imagine them attached to a spinning globe – at times one may be in full view, but it is only a matter of time before others come to the forefront again. It can be helpful to revisit the questions in the next practice time and time again.

Practice 12.2: Mindfulness right now!

Uncovering values

Give yourself an opportunity in your day to dedicate some time to this practice, free from distractions as much as possible – perhaps right now works? Have something to write on in front of you and allow these questions to enter in to your awareness as you jot down any thoughts that show up.

▶ Begin by bringing to mind someone who truly inspires you. This might be someone who you know or it might be someone you have never met before. Take a few minutes to write down what it is about this person that you admire. What personal qualities do they demonstrate that you consider important? What have they taught you that you want to remember? Once you have written some thoughts down, thank this person in your own mind for being such an inspiration to you.

▶ If you could choose to build any kind of friendship, what would it look like? How would you treat your friends if you could be the best friend imaginable?

▶ If you could be the ideal partner/daughter/son/father/mother/aunt/ uncle, what personal qualities would you want to develop and act by? How would you want to be with your loved ones, even during difficult times?

▶ If your education or career is important to you, consider what most sparks your passion and interest. Describe the type of worker you would most want to be.

▶ How would you, ideally, want to continue to grow and develop as a person, including what is important in terms of your physical and mental health? Consider how your own self-care can impact on all your other values.

▶ What else in your life provides moments of fun, relaxation and play? What does this suggest about how else you want to be as a person?

▶ How do you ideally want to be with yourself when you are facing challenges or struggling in some way? Is it important for you to be courageous, encouraging, non-judgemental, kind perhaps?

▶ What qualities about yourself do you already embody that are important to you?

How was that for you? We hope that this practice began to help you to reconnect with your heartfelt wish for how you want to live your life. It might be that it was difficult to think about some of these things, which is understandable, as so many of us busy people spend very little time reflecting on what matters most to us as we rush around trying to get everything done.

If it was challenging for you, then you might find it helpful to hear about some of the values that came to our minds when we did this practice. In terms of relationships, we valued things like being caring, respectful, supportive and loving, while for our own health we found that being self-compassionate, accepting, reflective and active were important to us.

We also recognised the importance of values like being playful and having fun, being assertive, open and patient. But these are just the values we chose when writing this book, and you may have chosen entirely different values, and that is great, we cannot all head down the same path!

For many people, there are a lot of different values that are important to them. You may have written down many in the previous practice. It can be difficult to hold all of these in mind at once, so we invite you to pick your top three or four that are the most important to you right now, perhaps highlighting them in some way so they stand out. Of course, these might change over time, but, for the next few practices, we invite you to bring your attention to these values.

Practice 12.3: I haven't got time for this!

Growing older

▶ Find a comfortable position and close your eyes or fix your gaze on a spot in front of you, if you prefer. Take a few moments to ground yourself, perhaps by bringing your attention to your breathing to anchor you in this present moment.

▶ Imagine going forward in time many years, seeing yourself grow older.

▶ Imagine too that you have lived those years completely inconsistently with your three or four chosen values. Imagine the kinds of things that might have got in the way of you living a life that really mattered to you (busyness, rushing around maybe?). Try to picture what your life might look like, what you would be doing or not doing and imagine what effect this would have on you.

▶ Notice what it is like to imagine this, noticing any thoughts and feelings that arise. Notice where you feel this most strongly in your body. Stay here for a few moments, allowing these thoughts and feelings to emerge.

▶ Take a deep breath and, as you exhale, allow this image to fade away.

▶ Now, imagine again that you have grown much older, but this time you have lived a life fully consistent with your values. Imagine what that would look like, the sorts of things you might have done and the effect it has had on your life.

▶ Notice what it is like to imagine this, noticing any thoughts and feelings that arise. Notice where you feel this most strongly in your body. Stay for a few moments, allowing these thoughts and feelings to emerge.

▶ Take a deep breath and, as you exhale, allow this image to fade away.

So, how was that for you? We are guessing that imagining the future acting inconsistently with your values brought up some uncomfortable thoughts and feelings. It is unlikely to be the kind of life you want, so we invite you to begin to consider how, right now, you can choose a different journey. In fact, in any given moment with mindfulness, you can choose to act in accordance with your values and get back on track to living the life you truly want and being the kind of person you really want to be. As always, the key here is present moment awareness (mindfulness).

Mindfulness and values

Mindfulness allows you to notice what you might be doing that is inconsistent with your values and it provides you with the opportunity to notice and check in with when you feel most alive, highlighting what matters most to you and what you value. Similarly, mindfulness allows you to notice when you are in pain, again indicating what is important to you. For example, the pain of loss around the ending of a relationship may remind you of your deeply held desire to be close and connected to another person. It also helps you to unhook from the life-limiting thoughts and struggles you may have with difficult feelings that might be leading you in the wrong direction, away from your values. With mindfulness you can respond more flexibly and effectively to these troublesome thoughts and feelings, making room for them, allowing you to pursue your values even when it feels effortful or scary to do that. Mindfulness helps you to keep on track and acting in line with what matters most to you in any specific moment and situation.

Practice 12.4: Mindfulness right now!

Following your heart

▶ Take each of your values in turn and write down a few small things you have done recently that are in line with this value. We suggest one or two for each, but more is fine, too. For example, if your value is being loving, you might recall a hug you gave your partner, sending a birthday card to a friend, asking a colleague how they are feeling today.

▶ Now take each of your values in turn but, this time, write down some small things you could do over the next month that are in line with this value. Again, we suggest about one or two for each.

▶ Now repeat the previous step, but this time think about things over the next week that you could do that would really bring your values to life.

▶ And now consider the same again, but for today. What could you do today that is in line with your values?

▶ Finally, just picking one of your values, what one thing could you do right now, in this very moment, that would express your heartfelt value? Would you be willing to give it a go then see what happens? Do it right now, before you read on.

I have no time for values!

We are not suggesting that you do even more things and fill your diary with lots of value-driven behaviours on top of your busy schedule, as you are likely just to become more busy, stressed and exhausted. But, perhaps it is time to ask yourself what is the most valuable way to spend your time (the answer to which may change in any given moment). For example, is it more valuable in this moment to spend longer in the office or spend time playing with the children? Everything you do, every minute you spend *doing* is your choice. How do you want to prioritise your time? If you do not have time for something, it is not because there is no time, it is because it is not a priority or, perhaps, it feels uncomfortable to do it.

Only you can truly notice moment by moment whether your choices, behaviour and actions are value-based or motivated by some other, perhaps fearful, part of you. You get to notice, you get to choose. Who do you want to *be* in this world?

Throughout this book, we have explained that you really do not need to change anything in your life to practise mindfulness. It is already with you in any moment of your day, whether you are busy or not. But with practice, many people we work with begin to realise that they do want to make some meaningful changes in their life, even simple or small ones, particularly when they begin to focus on their values.

Mindfulness top tips to-go

In this chapter, you have learned that it is helpful to:

▶ Acknowledge whether what you are doing in any given moment is in the direction you really want to head.

▶ Understand that your values are chosen entirely by you and no one else.

▶ Explore ways of *being* rather than adding more and more on to your to-do list.

▶ Connect with who and what is truly important to you.

▶ Commit to making small steps towards what is most important to you.

▶ Consider prioritising your time based on your values, rather than squeezing more in and feeling increasingly busier and stressed.

CHAPTER

13

Mindfulness in the real world

So, here we are, in the final chapter to this book. Perhaps you are wondering if this mindfulness is working or not? Can you master it? Is it clicking into place? Any feeling is fine, really (just acknowledge it, there it is). Know that you can go right back to the start whenever you want or any other chapter that you desire (we hope that you will continue to revisit parts of this book) over and over again. Be aware that, just like this book, your awareness is not going anywhere; you can be aware whenever you want. Mindfulness is always with you, there is the opportunity to be mindful in any given moment, and we hope that, by now, you are starting to see that.

Awareness is abundant

Let us remind ourselves of this abundant awareness. The Western, or Westernised, modern world in which most of us live today is hectic, demanding and relentless. With endless advancements in technology, unsteady economies, worrisome politics and terrorism to contend with, we also attempt to balance time for work, friendships, relationships, children and 'leisure' time, to take care of money, families, housing, health and mental well-being, and somehow remain relatively sane most of the time.

This is combined with living alongside the realities faced by any living being, the fundamental suffering that we all experience, of ageing, illness and death. Even in the absence of anything exceptionally difficult in our lives, and especially when things are tough, it is an absolute miracle that there are still smiling faces, birthday celebrations, loving embraces and many random acts of kindness and generosity occurring every minute of every day.

We have an absolute abundance of these opportunities to become more aware of and it seems vital that we create more of this kind of space for ourselves. To be alive to this moment, to give it our attention, is to make it grow, and life can begin to transform from one of lack (where we may not be noticing much, we are half asleep or consumed with unhelpful narratives about the past or future) to one of blessings, rich and fertile, the good and not so good, our life becomes *alive.*

> There are only two days in the year that nothing can be done. One is called yesterday and the other is called tomorrow, so today is the right day to love, believe, do and mostly live.
>
> **Dalai Lama**

The great thing is that, if we miss this moment, we have another opportunity, the next moment, and then again and again and again, even when doing household chores!

This next practice can be done with any household task. You can transform your home and yourself with mindfulness. You may like to undertake this practice in the spirit of kindness, allowing yourself to take time to notice each movement as you dedicate it to your housemates, children, partner or any other being (such as yourself). This way, you now have a good few minutes transformed from mumbling under your breath about the inequalities of menial domestic chore distribution into a tranquil oasis of benevolence.

Practice 13.1: I haven't got time for this!

Mindful washing up

▶ Take a moment to enjoy the bubbles sitting in the warm water or watch the tap like a waterfall cascading into the sink. Notice the sensations around you of colours, sounds and smells.

▶ Treat each dish as precious; as an opportunity to delight in this moment. Just washing each dish slowly, with care and attention.

▶ Use the breath to bring you back to the moment if your mind wanders. Allow yourself to pause with the cleaning of the dishes and just breathe in once, out once. Now return gently to the task.

▶ Allow yourself to become alive to the moment through your senses.

▶ As you wash up, cleaning each item with care, let your thoughts (like 'it is not fair, I do everything around here' or whatever else they may be) dissolve in the washing-up water along with the dirt from the plates, cups and cutlery.

▶ Be fully present in this act of kindness.

Awareness is the part of your mind that does not change for the entirety of your lifespan; it is always there, often in the background as you rush around contending with your busy life. Your busy existence and the world around you changes, but your awareness that notices these changes never changes – it remains constant and the same. Your awareness has been with you since the day you were born and will be with you until the end of your time. It is always with you in every moment, it is with you right here and right now as you read the final pages of this book (as it was when you started to read this book and it will be again when you come to revisit it later). Let us not lose touch with it any more.

Practice 13.2: Mindfulness right now!

Awareness is now

Take just a moment again now to tune into that experience of awareness:

▶ Notice the sensations of holding this book (or e-reader, or whatever device you may be reading this on). The weight, textures. And who is it that is noticing the sensations of holding the book?

▶ Perhaps also notice any particular thoughts arising, any emotions or urges to move or other sensations. And who is it that is noticing those thoughts, emotions and urges?

▶ If *you* are noticing these sensations, thoughts, emotions and urges, then you cannot also be these sensations, thoughts, emotions and urges.

▶ You are much larger than these experiences.

It is likely that, as you read this right now, you no longer are aware of the sensations of holding the book (e-reader or whatever device) that we asked you to focus on just a moment ago in the last exercise – this is because you are now paying attention to what you are reading. This awareness also reminds us that all the experiences that you have, whether in the form of a thought produced by your mind, a physical sensation or emotion experienced in your body, an urge or a way of behaving or acting will always come and go again, as if they were clouds passing by in the sky of your 'awareness'. We can now appreciate the futility of grasping at these experiences and how impossible it is to get anywhere from doing so, except possibly more stressed, busier and exhausted.

Nevertheless, we do need to engage some degree of effort to focus our attention on the present, particularly in very challenging circumstances or when these ideas are quite new. This effort is not about attaining the prize for the biggest mindfulness powers ever, it is more about the effort of letting go and reminding ourselves that, even if we had such a prize, it would not make us happy, better or safer anyway. You already hold the answer to all your problems, keep observing, dropping into awareness and this will become clearer to you.

> You, the richest person in the world, have been working and struggling endlessly, not understanding that you already possess what you seek.

The Lotus Sutra

Here is another quick mindfulness practice that you can try every day (or most days, we hope!) without having to change your daily routine – this time it is in the shower or bath. It will help you recognise that your awareness is here with you, even when you are busy getting ready for the day. It will allow you to get out of your head, to really enjoy your shower/bath time and wake up to the rich experience that it can be.

Practice 13.3: I haven't got time for this!

It's time for a scrub down!

▶ Notice the sound of the water as it sprays out of the shower head, as it lands on different surfaces, like your body, the tiles, shower screen or as it runs down the plug hole.

▶ Notice the sensation of water, its pressure hitting against your head, your different body parts; the temperature of the water against your body. Notice how this feels.

▶ Notice the smell of the soap and the shampoo.

▶ Notice how the soap and shampoo feel against your skin and how it feels as they wash away.

▶ Notice the water droplets on the walls or shower screen and dripping down your body.

▶ Notice the steam rising and filling the shower, the room.

▶ Should any thoughts show up about what you are doing, or anything else at all, just acknowledge these thoughts, let go of them and bring your attention back to your experience of the shower.

▶ Who would have guessed that, without all those thoughts crowding in with you (maybe about the boss/car mechanic/Donald Trump), your shower could be so spacious!

It's not working

So, how do we know that mindfulness is working and what do we do when it is not? Well, our answer is, just breathe, try it, see for yourself. How is this very moment? Now, this one? Can you let the future unfold like this? Can you let go of having to control the outcome, can you trust yourself this much?

When we focus too much on the outcome (*when will this mindfulness thing work?*) we are not here in the present but rather there (or then!). Worrying whether mindfulness is or is not working is only going to stress you out right here and right now. Is that you trying to work it all out again, desperately trying to get it right, using mindfulness as a 'control' strategy to ensure you get to that perfect place of bliss? If so, notice this temptation for the mind to jump back in to its thinking/problem-solving mode.

As we outlined at the start of this book, if we develop an attitude of openness (acceptance) as to whether we do or do not reap the benefits of mindfulness, we are in a much better place to notice the fortunate by-products of regular practice arising, naturally. Flowers open without us forcing the buds and we can also trust that things will happen at the right time, naturally. This is about coming to appreciate and live with the 'what is' rather than the 'what if?'

The truth is that all the benefits of mindfulness that you want are already within you – you are already relaxed, efficient, creative, an excellent decision maker, productive and at peace – it is all there and working just fine, but fretting that this stuff will never come, that is what gets in the way of this and clouds your vision to this reality.

You get there by realizing that you are already there.

Eckhart Tollee – author

Practice 13.4: I haven't got time for this!

The Goldilocks principle

Try the following when difficulties arise with being mindful as you go about your busy days. So, if you are finding that:

- It is too hard – yes, and this is a moment that is hard, be mindful, breathe, this too shall pass.
- I do not understand – yes, and this is a moment that is confusing, nothing to work out, nothing to fix.
- I cannot do it – yes, and this is a moment of struggling, nothing to get 'right', just as it is.
- I am so happy, I just could not practise – yes, and this is a moment of happiness, breathe, this too shall pass.
- I am so miserable, I just could not practise – yes, a moment of unhappiness, breathe and let go.
- I am really good at this, I have got it! I do not need to practise any more – a moment of clarity, this too shall pass.
- This mindfulness porridge is too hot, too cold or (shock, horror) all gone! This moment, whatever it is, is as it is, nothing more, nothing less.

Through letting go (of attempts to change what is already here), you will find relaxation, calm, spaciousness, contentment, ease and peace. Mindfulness is a skill that you can bring to any of life's problems and it will bring you positive results. Let go and see for yourself.

Wow, this is great!

When you abide in the moment, in your awareness, life's richness is revealed. At times, mindfulness can give us clarity, awareness and insight with the speed and precision of a lightning bolt and it can knock us off our feet.

Often, mindfulness is a clumsy affair, we notice something and then drift back to our habits, then we realise this, and promptly do it again. As you know by now, though, this does get more instinctive, and the quality of experience can become a little subtler. With practice, we recognise the nuances of our own mind's little habits, its particular hamster qualities and foibles.

Periods of ease can become gradually prolonged as we are now attentive to life's usual pitfalls and, when we fall off the wagon, we realise that there was not really a wagon to fall from anyway, and sitting on our posterior in the dirt is just where we happen to be right now.

> Life just offers what it offers, and our task is to bow to it, to meet it with understanding and compassion. There are no laurels to acquire.
>
> **Jack Kornfield – author**

Yes, you guessed it; this is an ongoing journey for us all. Mindfulness is not to be attained and completed, no certificates will be awarded here. It is a practice for life, in and out of awareness we go, cultivating and reinforcing the same. And it is all so very worth it.

Some of the most common utterances that we hear from our busy clients are: *I don't need to practise right now, I feel great! Why is this not working, I'm so stressed and it's just not helping.* Or *It's just so difficult to practise, I keep forgetting!* We understand why we might not feel the urge to practise when all is rosy in the garden, why fix something if it ain't broke, hey? We get this, we are the same. But, what is your purpose in taking your car to the garage for an MOT we would ask?

Mindfulness is not just for the stressful times, it is a way of being that, if you practise (when you are feeling fine and dandy too), will help you out when you need it the most. So, do not expect it to magically appear or work a treat when you feel like the world is crashing down around you and you cannot see a way out. It is a discipline – practise, practise, practise is the key. But know that it does get easier and, before you know it, awareness will arise more naturally and with more clarity and frequency.

Try not to see mindfulness as yet another set of garden shears that is pulled out annually from the cobwebs of the garden shed to extract those pesky weeds – you may find that they are a bit rusty and too blunt. Nurture your awareness every day, as much as you can (even with just a few mindful breaths) and that way you will find that it is more naturally to hand when your garden is overgrown and those bothersome nettles need attending to. Likewise, when the sun is out and the flowers are in full bloom, you will find that you notice this, and may even take time to sit back with a beer in the deckchair and soak it all up.

It may feel strange, frustrating, and the rest, at first (and then again) when practising this new way of being – but remember that this is absolutely normal and these experiences are a gateway to mindfulness, too. Peace, relaxation and well-being are products of the mindfulness work that you do. Try to focus on them less and they will arise more naturally.

Practice 13.5: Mindfulness right now!

What is showing up?

Over time, as you have continued to practise regularly, have you noticed the following:

▶ Clarity of mind, improved concentration and focus?

▶ A greater sense of ease, peace, relaxation, stability (despite how busy you are)?

▶ A greater sense of productivity, efficiency with your daily tasks?

▶ Improved communication in your relationships?

▶ You are more free to make the choices that move you towards the life you want?

And, if you have not, then let it go, do not worry about it – be mindful . . . and then, as soon as you do this, as sure as night follows day – there you have it: clarity, freedom, peace and tranquillity (and then they, too, pass again, and return, and pass . . .).

Our busy world in all its glory

We have illustrated to you how being busy without reflection, awareness and mindful attention is the cause of more busyness and stress in our lives. Busyness on its own is not the problem here – it is our relationship to it. When we carry on with our busyness, 'blissfully' unaware, ignorant to our ability to be aware, we miss out on so much of our life, causing ourselves more stress, busyness and taking less satisfaction from it all; we lose sight of our true purpose.

We live in a world that is stressful and painful; you will be busy, you will experience heartache, loss, fear and stress if you are choosing to take part in this thing we call life. The choice is yours. Know that if you are not willing to make room for and lean in to your suffering then you will not really be taking part at all and all your efforts to escape what you do not want will lead to more suffering.

For too long we have assumed that the answer to our pain is to work it out, to problem-solve and push it away – hit the 'feel good' button and keep it firmly held down in place. But we are only kidding ourselves with this and we continue to buy into this farce via the media, Hollywood and new technology. We work on this premise – that we must feel good and not feel bad, but working towards not feeling bad just really equates to not feeling at all! You know this by now and that this does not work – there is no way out of your pain, only a way into it and that is how to truly gain genuine freedom and relief.

The truth is that we cannot change the way the modern world is and the experiences we will have as we bustle through it. When you reject your experiences, your feelings, your suffering, you are truly rejecting yourself – your feelings and experiences become disowned and lost. Are you really prepared to turn away from yourself, no matter how hard it might be to face this suffering, in your hour of need? We cannot guarantee anyone else will be there for us, even with their best intentions. But you are right there and have been all along, you are still with yourself now. If not you, then who? If not now, then when?

It is important to offer yourself this kindness and mindful compassion if you want some warmth, care and stability (even if it is just for one moment) amidst this often cold, judgemental and hostile world. That is how you might make this stressful experience that much more bearable, more satisfying and manageable and come to experience all of it in all its glory.

Practice 13.6: Mindfulness right now!

Willing and able

The questions to ask yourself are:

▶ Am I willing to step into my life experience and fully engage with it all?

▶ Am I willing to take all this busy world has to offer along with me for the ride?

▶ Can I let go of the 'what if?' and see the 'what is'?

▶ Am I willing to hold my pain and suffering with dignity?

▶ Am I willing to invite my pain in, take care of it and pay it kind attention?

▶ Am I willing to act boldly, move towards a valued life, even when it feels so difficult to do so?

▶ What do I offer myself, this world, if I run away from my experiences right now?

▶ What is my purpose here, right now?

Now is the time to wake up and wise up

Our human mind did not evolve for this modern world. It was designed to protect us, to take in as much information as it could, to second-guess our downfall, to see the worst around us, to problem-solve – yes, we will survive! Yet, in these modern times, we have information flying at us from every direction all the time at an alarming rate. We like to multitask. Most of us are plugged into one or more devices at the same time, checking emails while surfing the web, following the Jones' on Twitter, TV on in the background, music playing in our headphones, answering texts on our phone – oh and yes, dear, how was your day?

We have so much to process and a lot of this information is scary stuff, too. You only have to turn on the TV, log into the news, open a newspaper for a few minutes to hear and read all about the cataclysmic disasters, death tolls rising and global infections that are out to get us. Our minds are programmed to work all this out, to fret to protect us in the face of such hazards and catastrophe. Like a computer, our minds are ready for the next upload of data, all too happy to fill up any empty space with the next constant barrage of pain and suffering to work out. We then lose ourselves; we lose contact with who we are, with others, sucking in all this information overload, in our attempts to keep safe and sound. Oh, the irony – we then become psychologically exhausted, burnt out and distressed. It is not surprising that an escape to another peaceful place and time begins to sound very attractive indeed.

We then need to cultivate minds that are ready and allow us to cope with this world: our very own splendid creation. We need to offer ourselves back this gift, create a place in this world, a place to stand within it, to feel firm and strong amidst the crazy busyness and stress that we continue to bombard ourselves with. Let us wake up and be kind to ourselves – allow ourselves to truly enjoy this new wonderful creation of ours; the modern world – mindfulness is this place within which we can stand.

The awareness gained through mindfulness is the space within which we can then create more space. This space is large enough to hold it all; the crazy busyness, the peaceful stillness, the grief, the joy, the hamster mind, the man made of stardust, the smartphone and tablet, the whole universe and the kitchen sink – all of it.

Practice 13.7: I haven't got time for this!

Mind the gap

▶ Look in front of you and choose an object to pay attention to for a moment. If it's a very large object, perhaps notice a small part of it.

▶ Notice the colours, the textures, the shape and size of the object.

▶ Notice that the object is over *there* and you are over *here*. Notice the space between you and the object.

▶ Now close your eyes and notice the sensations in your left foot.

▶ Perhaps you notice the sensation of heat or the weight of your foot pulled towards the ground.

▶ Notice that the sensations in your foot are over *there and* you are over *here*. Allow yourself to experience the space between you and the object of your attention, your foot.

Keeping going

You might find that, whilst reading this book, there have been times when you have been practising mindfulness and other times when you have had a break from practising it. It can be challenging to keep returning to practising it, especially when our natural instincts tell us to fight or run away from what is uncomfortable, effortful or challenging in the present. It is highly likely that there will be many, many times your mind pulls you away from the practices. But, if we can return to practising as much as we can, then a deeper confidence can grow, a confidence that says, 'I can handle whatever life deals me.'

It can be helpful to create a space in your home dedicated for mindfulness. Choose somewhere where there is the least chance for distraction. You might choose a space on the floor, which you could make more comfortable with blankets and cushions, or if you prefer to, you might have a comfy chair to use. You might choose to place plants or candles around to create a space that feels more tranquil. You might also keep a pen and paper nearby to write down any reflections after your practice. Once your mindfulness space is created, you might make a commitment to use it and do this next simple practice there at least once a day.

Practice 13.8: Mindfulness right now!

Mindful silence

Read through the following instructions before setting a timer on your phone or an alarm clock for five or ten minutes.

- ▶ Focus your attention on the sensations of breathing.
- ▶ Let go of any thoughts, feelings, other sensations that might arise as you return your attention back to the sensations and rhythm of breathing, time and time again.
- ▶ When the timer stops, open your eyes, carrying with you a mindful intention throughout the rest of your day,

The mindful warrior (*not* worrier!)

Can you continue to take with you what you have learned from this book into your real world? Can you find your inner strength, lean into your wise and abundantly spacious mind and let it help you find the way? Can you live boldly and continue to do what you care about, what is important to you with courage alongside the pain that you might feel when doing it? You mindful warrior, you!

The choice is yours. We hope that we have helped you to see, to experience how strong and powerful you really are, how you have all the answers to a less busy and more peaceful life inside you already. Look inwards – there you are.

Your vision will become clear when you look into your heart. Who looks outside, dreams. Who looks inside, awakens.

Carl Jung

Using mindfulness enables us to create space from our busyness and stress, meeting them also with understanding and compassion and bowing with awareness. Practising mindfulness, with intention, is a way in which we can train our minds to return to awareness, which is our natural and authentic state of being.

In the end, these things matter most: How well did you love? How fully did you live? How deeply did you let go?

Gautama Buddha

Mindfulness top tips to-go

In this chapter, you have learned that it is helpful to:

▶ Know that awareness is the key to finding some space and tranquillity in these increasingly hectic modern times.

▶ Recognise that we have an abundance of opportunities to become more aware in this Westernised world.

▶ Try to focus your attention when times are tough and mindfulness is new to you.

▶ Try not to worry whether mindfulness is working or when it will work, as this only takes you away from now and only will stress you out.

▶ Remember, mindfulness is not just for the stressful times, but is best practised when you are feeling fine; that way, it will be to hand when you need it the most.

▶ Recognise that we have all the tools to practise mindfulness already, with us right here and right now.

▶ Simply be *busy* without adding more busyness and stress on top of that.

Tracking your practice

In Part 5, we have begun to connect mindfully with our values and we have encouraged you to take steps towards what matters most to you in your life. We have also ended by exploring how you might continue on with your own personal journey of mindfulness. We encourage you to explore the exercises below that you feel comfortable with and then return to any of the other previous practices that have caught your interest.

Practice	Page	When?	Notes
12.1: To-be list	185	Ask these questions at the start of each day or as frequently as you can.	
12.2: Uncovering values	186	Return to these questions when you have lost direction in life or as often as you want to.	
12.4: Following your heart	189	Return to these questions when you have lost direction in life or as often as you want to.	
13.1: Mindful washing-up	195	Whenever you are doing the washing-up or any other household chore at all.	
13.2: Awareness is now	196	Any moment you notice you are on autopilot – how about right now?	
13.3: It's time for a scrub down	197	Whenever you take a shower or bath.	

You may wish to now (if you have not already) look up the audio files of guided practices that accompany this book at:

www.pearson-books.com/mindfulness

We do hope that you have enjoyed reading this book as much as we have enjoyed writing it. We wish you well on your journey ahead. May you experience joy, may you experience peace and may you experience a rich and meaningful life.

> By sharing something, I realized that I'm not alone, that there are a lot of people that share with me the same preoccupations, the same ideas, the same ideals, and the same quest for a meaning for this life.

Paulo Coelho – author

Recommended reading

▷ Alidin, S. (2010) *Mindfulness for Dummies*. John Wiley & Sons: West Sussex

▷ Alidin, S. (2015) *The Mindful Way through Stress: The Proven 8-Week Path to Health, Happiness, and Well-Being*. Guildford Press: New York

▷ Bond, F.W., Flaxman, P.E., Livheim, F. and Hayes, S.C. (2013) *The Mindful and Effective Employee: An Acceptance and Commitment Therapy Training Manual for Improving Well-Being and Performance*. New Harbinger: California

▷ Brach, T. (2003) *Radical Acceptance: Embracing your Life with the Heart of a Buddha*. Bantam: New York

▷ Dalai Lama (1999) *Ancient Wisdom, Modern World: Ethics for A New Millennium*. Little, Brown and Company: London

▷ Deschene, L. (2015) *Tiny Buddha's 365 Tiny Love Challenges*. Harper-Collins: New York

▷ Forsyth, J. and Eifert, G. (2016) *The Mindfulness and Acceptance Workbook for Anxiety: A Guide to Breaking Free from Anxiety, Phobias, and Worry Using Acceptance and Commitment Therapy*. New Harbinger: California

▷ Gerhardt, S. (2004) *Why Love Matters: How Affection Shapes a Baby's Brain*. Routledge: London

▷ Germer, C.K. (2009) *The Mindful Path to Self-Compassion: Freeing Yourself from Destructive Thoughts and Emotions*. Guildford Press: New York

▷ Gilbert, P. (2010) *The Compassionate Mind*. Constable & Robinson: London

▷ Gilbert, P. and Choden (2013) *Mindful Compassion*. Robinson: London

▷ Harris, R. (2008) *The Happiness Trap: Based on ACT: A Revolutionary Mindfulness-based Programme for Overcoming Stress, Anxiety and Depression*. Robinson: London

▷ Harris, R. (2012) *The Reality Slap: How to Find Fulfilment When Life Hurts*. Constable & Robinson: London

▷ Hayes, S.C. and Smith, S. (2005) *Get Out of Your Mind and Into Your Life: The New Acceptance and Commitment Therapy*. New Harbinger: California

▷ Kabat-Zinn, J. (2004) *Wherever You Go, There You Are: Mindfulness Meditation for Everyday Life*. Piaktus: London

▶ Kornfield, J. (2000) *After the Ecstasy, the Laundry: How the Heart Grows Wise on the Spiritual Path.* Bantam Books: New York

▶ Kolts, R and Chodron, T. (2013) *Living with an Open Heart: How to cultivate compassion in everyday life.* Robinson: London

▶ Leonoard-Curtin, A and Leonard-Curtin, T. (2017) *The Power of Small: Making tiny but powerful changes when everything feels too much.* Hachette Books: Ireland

▶ Neff, K. (2011) *Self-Compassion: Stop Beating Yourself Up and Leave Insecurity Behind.* HarperCollins: New York

▶ Oliver, J., Hill, J. and Morris, E. (2015) *Activate Your Life: Using Acceptance and Mindfulness to Build a Life that is Rich, Fulfilling and Fun.* Robinson: London

▶ Salzberg, S. (2004) *Loving Kindness: The Revolutionary Art of Happiness.* Shambhala Publications: Boston, MA

▶ Sinclair, M. and Beadman, M. (2016) *The Little ACT Workbook. An Introduction to Acceptance and Commitment Therapy: A Mindfulness-Based Guide for Living a Full and Meaningful Life.* Crimson Publishing: Bath, UK

▶ Sinclair, M. and Seydel, J. (2016) *Working with Mindfulness: Keeping Calm and Focused to Get the Job Done.* Pearson: Harlow

▶ Suzuki, S. (1973) *Zen Mind, Beginner's Mind.* Weatherhill: New York

▶ The Mindfulness Project (2015) *I Am Here Now: A creative mindfulness guide and journal.* Ebury Press: London

▶ Teasdale, J., Williams, M. and Segal, Z. (2014) *The Mindful Way Workbook: An 8-week program to free yourself from depression and emotional distress.* Guilford Press: New York

▶ Tich Nhat Hanh (1991) *The Miracle of Mindfulness: An Introduction to the Practice of Meditation.* Rider Books: London

▶ Tolle, E. (2004) *The Power of Now: A Guide To Spiritual Enlightenment.* New World Library: San Francisco

▶ Welford, M. (2012) *The Compassionate Mind Approach to Building Self-Confidence.* Robinson: London

▶ Welford, M. (2016) *Compassion Focused Therapy for Dummies.* John Wiley & Sons: West Sussex

▶ Williams, M. and Penman, D. (2011) *Mindfulness: A Practical Guide to Finding Peace in a Frantic World.* Piaktus: London

▶ Wilson, K.G. and DuFrene, T. (2010) *Things Might Go Terribly, Horribly Wrong: A guide to life liberated from anxiety.* New Harbinger: California.

Further useful contacts, resources and support

- ACT Companion, The Happiness Trap app with Dr Russ Harris: **www.actcompanion.com**
- Action for Happiness, information, courses and events: **www.actionforhappiness.org**
- Bangor Centre for Mindfulness Practice and Research, mindfulness training, practice and research: **www.bangor.ac.uk/mindfulness**
- BeMindful, information, resources and online mindfulness course: **www.bemindful.co.uk**
- Breathing Zone, app for guided breathing exercises: **www.breathing.zone**
- Buddist Geeks, information on mindfulness, Buddhism, talks and events – also has podcasts to download: **www.buddhistgeeks.com**
- Centre for Compassion Focused Therapy, New York: **www.mindfulcompassion.com**
- City Psychology Group, mindfulness workshops, mindfulness-based therapy: **www.city-psychology.co.uk**
- Compassionate Mind, information and resources based on compassion and mindfulness: **www.compassionatemind.net**
- Dharma Seed, downloadable talks and information about retreats: **www.dharmaseed.org**
- Everyday Mindfulness, information, resources, courses and blogs: **www.everyday-mindfulness.org**
- Franklin Covey (Live with Purpose), define values and build a mission statement for a purposeful life: **https://msb.franklincovey.com**
- Gaia House, retreat centre, Devon: **www.gaiahouse.co.uk**
- Headspace, mindfulness app: **www.headspace.com/ headspace-meditation-app**
- Insight Timer, free mindfulness app: **www.insighttimer.com**
- Institut De Psychologie Contextuelle, therapy, training and consulting for organizations and individuals: www.contextpsy.com
- Martin Wilks, mindfulness retreats: **www.martinwilks.com/ mindfulness-retreats**

▶ Mindful, up-to-date information on mindfulness, a magazine, newsletter, guided practices and blogs: **www.mindful.org**

▶ Mindful Creation, mindfulness app information on mindfulness and practices: **www.mindfulcreation.com**

▶ Mindfulness Bell, free, downloadable mindfulness bell for your PC or laptop: **www.mindfulnessdc.org/bell/index.html**

▶ Mindfulnet, independent mindfulness information website and resources: **www.mindfulnet.org**

▶ Moulin de Chaves, retreat centre, France: **www.moulindechaves.org**

▶ Mrs Mindfulness, information, blogs, courses and retreats: **www.mrsmindfulness.com**

▶ Oxford Centre for Mindfulness, Mindfulness training and courses, resources and research: **www.oxfordmindfulness.org**

▶ Plum Village, retreat centre, France: **www.plumvillage.org**

▶ Rick Hanson, mindfulness newsletter, practices, videos and podcasts and much more: **www.rickhanson.net**

▶ Spirit Rock, retreat centre, USA: **www.spiritrock.org**

▶ The Act Matrix Academy, webinars and consultations: **www.theactmatrixacademy.com**

▶ The Barn Retreat, retreat centre, Devon: **www.sharphamtrust.org/ The-Barn-Retreat**

▶ The Compassionate Mind Foundation, information, workshops and conferences on the compassion-focussed approach: **www.compassionatemind.co.uk**

▶ The Foundations of Well-being, a year-long programme for developing happiness, love and resilience with leading experts: **www.thefoundationsofwellbeing.com**

▶ The Free Mindfulness Project, free downloadable practices, information, resources, courses, apps and blogs: **www.freemindfulness.org**

▶ The Good Project (Values-Sort Activity), useful information on values and a tool for identifying values: **www.thegoodproject.org/toolkits-curricula/the-goodwork-toolkit/value-sort-activity/**

▶ The Happiness Trap, online 8 week program to improve genuine happiness: **www.thehappinesstrap.com/8-week-program**

▶ The Mindfulness Summit, talks and tutorials from leading experts in mindfulness: **www.themindfulnesssummit.com**

▶ Tiny Buddha, information, resources, blogs and forum: **www.tinybuddha.com**

Index

INDEX